Criminal Actions and Social Situations

Anthony Amatrudo

Criminal Actions and Social Situations

Understanding the Role of Structure and Intentionality

palgrave
macmillan

Anthony Amatrudo
Law School
Middlesex University
London, UK

ISBN 978-1-137-45730-1   ISBN 978-1-137-45731-8   (eBook)
https://doi.org/10.1057/978-1-137-45731-8

Library of Congress Control Number: 2017961835

Cover illustration: Baranovskaya

Printed on acid-free paper

This Palgrave Macmillan imprint is published by Springer Nature
The registered company is Macmillan Publishers Ltd.
The registered company address is: The Campus, 4 Crinan Street, London, N1 9XW, United Kingdom

"Innocence is like a dumb leper who has lost his bell, wandering the world, meaning no harm."

Greene, G. (1973) The Quiet American. Heinemann & Bodley Head: London.

Acknowledgements

My thanks are due to St Edmund's College, Cambridge and the Institute of Criminology in Cambridge who have both supported my work for many years. Sir Anthony Bottoms FBA, I must thank, for the usefully open-ended questions he proffered at a paper I gave at the Institute of Criminology in late 2016 and which have certainly informed the text in this book. I am grateful to the Max-Planck Institute for Foreign and International Criminal Law in Freiburg and the Max-Planck Institute for European Legal History in Frankfurt am Main who have for several years supported my research with various visiting fellowships and opened their amazing resources to me. The friendly scholarly community at both the Frankfurt *Planck* and the Freiburg *Planck* have been great supports. I am also grateful for the assistance extended to me by the University of Basel where I spent many useful hours in its state of the art library. My publisher, Palgrave Macmillan, has been very professional and supportive throughout this project. My personal thanks for friendship and inspiration go to: Hans-Jorg Albrecht; Blackheath Rugby Club; Leslie Blake; Jake and Dinos Chapman; John Charvet; Antje du Bois Pedain; Robert Fine; the denizens of the Groucho Club; Volker Grundies; Felicia Herrschaft; Andreas von Hirsch; Jennifer Kessler; Ronnie Lippens; Sarah Lucas; Steven Lukes FBA; David Polizzi; Marc Quinn; Robert Reiner; Magnus Ryan; George Steiner FBA and Colin Sumner. The words of the late Brian Barry FBA, who I had the enormous privilege of working with as a research student at the LSE I recall daily; only now realising their true wisdom.

Thanks also to the *Onati Socio-Legal Series* for permission to make use of an earlier version of an article for this book: Amatrudo, A. (2016) "Applying Analytical Reasoning to Clarify Intention and Responsibility in Joint Enterprise Cases." *The Politics and Jurisprudence of Group Offending: Onati Socio-Legal Series* (2016) 6 (4) pp. 920–936.

Max-Planck Institute for European Legal History   Anthony Amatrudo
Hansaallee, Frankfurt, Germany
8th August 2017

Contents

Section 1

Technical and Analytical Considerations

1

The Central Problem of Collective Action

The basic issue this book seeks to address is the knotty problem of what exactly collective action is. In this regard it is more ambitious and more broadly focused than is typical for a work focused upon Criminology. The job of this chapter is to move the existing criminological settlement around gangs, and joint enterprise, towards a more technical concentration upon the nature of individual action and its relationship with joint action. In doing this I largely follow the line I originally set out in my earlier article (Amatrudo 2016). My view is that it is a more straightforward task to seek to apportion criminal responsibility *technically* than to use the current, overly simplified and culturally reductive, accounts. This more technical approach makes the allocation of culpability surer. The argument will be that the law ought to be focused upon the wilful actions of individuals acting either alone or in a group. Individuals commit crimes, though they often do so with others. Culpability can only reside with individuals and their individual actions and with groups that are comprised of individuals. Culpability is only incidentally a structural matter. Whilst robbers, street gang members, war criminals, drug dealers and the like may form a group, what really matters are the individual actions of actors even where there is agreement about the intentional

© The Author(s) 2018
A. Amatrudo, *Criminal Actions and Social Situations*,
https://doi.org/10.1057/978-1-137-45731-8_1

status of the group. The individual who stabs with a knife is always more culpable than the person who looked on. Furthermore, serious consideration needs to be afforded to goal setting, intentionality and deliberation when considering the criminal action of criminal actors; more so than the role of culture. When such technical matters are marginalised, the legitimacy of the outcome becomes inadequate, as is seen in the rise of joint enterprise prosecutions since the 1980s in the UK (Williams and Clarke 2016). Our aim will be to better understand the actions, deliberations and goals of individuals, and of groups, simply because these individuals are held responsible for their actions. Accordingly, we must deconstruct the blasé arguments often advanced concerning joint criminal activity in order to weigh more carefully the elements that make it up. We can all agree that it is certainly possible for individuals to act *with a common purpose*: whilst also understanding that such a claim is a very complicated, and multi-faceted, determination to make.

On the matter of culpability we must allow that one of most important elements in collective action is the understanding that individuals, themselves, may self-impose certain constraints upon their deliberation in the form of goals and intentions. Collective action is simply what we call the outcome of what happens when all the members of a given group accept the same constraints put on their personal deliberations in order that they might bring about collectively acceptable outcomes or an array of collectively acceptable outcomes. We note that such an understanding is effectively *individualistic* since it holds that each member of the group makes their own personal deliberation. The only real difference between the deliberation of personal goals and collective ones is in terms of the sorts of goals that are set. The point here is that collective goals always rest upon the role of *individual* moral agency. Consequently, we should stress the role of individuals: rather than marginalise them in stressing collective agency. The personal responsibility of actors cannot be subsumed into merely an aspect of a broader ontological affiliation.

Any account of collective action has to do several things. It first has to explain how collective actions are themselves related to collective goals whilst noting that the collective is always comprised of individual actors and that is a tricky determination. Laws need to understand that the criminal responsibility of groups always comprises a degree of individual responsibility. It has been argued that: "There is no need to speak of degrees of responsibility. All that is required is the minimum voluntariness: that the person could have done otherwise" (Amatrudo 2010). Moreover, the responsibility of individuals, for their actions, cannot be waived or reduced to some minor aspect of some prior association with a group of other individuals. A useful way of understanding group membership is in terms of its connection to collective action. What is more we should note that groups can, and do, participate in collective actions that are wholly irrational and undertake activities that are immoral for the group and the individuals who make it up. We see this clearly in a lot of criminal activity, such as drug usage. It is an aspect of our world and of our nature. The drug gang deals drugs and though that is socially undesirable it is just another case of collective action. It is useful for criminologists to understand criminal activity as just a different sort of behaviour, or if you like action. There is no need to be censorious or to claim a form of exceptionalism for criminal action. Criminals are persons and can be simply understood as such. They act at times rationally and at other times irrationally and their actions are differentiated only by the fact that they breach a criminal threshold. When we determine their actions it is better done as a calm, moral and rational activity of reasoning and not as one that prioritises a disputed notion of culture. We need not ask if collective actions, whether criminal or not, are positive or not, in order to account for them. All the same it is useful here to look briefly at rational choice making in terms of the, so-called, prisoner's dilemma. List and Petit have looked at the prisoner's dilemma in relation to group agency. The prisoner's dilemma sets out to explain cooperative behaviour and how to assuage the costs of it, notably in terms of defecting. Essentially the prisoner's dilemma demonstrates that defection is often less costly than a strategy of straightforward cooperation for individuals. The prisoner's dilemma illustrates two important issues: (1) that there are cases of genuinely cooperative collective behaviour that seem not to correspond with the wellbeing of the cooperating parties and (2) that it is the case that individuals often justify their part in collective actions in terms of advancing a collective goal and can understand collective action as rational. Prisoner's dilemma games illustrate how individuals can undertake cooperative behaviour, as a rational activity, though they themselves may have good reasons not to engage in collective action. This may seem perplexing but the thing to note here is that there can be a range of reasons for individuals to undertake cooperative actions. Simply put collective actions in the prisoner's dilemma game illustrate that these may be justified in terms of the meta-reasoning of the collective action itself or as a justification for the individual in terms of their part in the collective action by way of executing an action that contributes to the greater collective action. In other words, collective action is commonplace and there is rational justification for those undertaking it. One may imagine collective actions which have no deliberative aspect to them, and possibly dancing might be such a case, whilst conceding that deliberation is usually an aspect of collective action. Those individuals who undertake collective action surely need to reason concerning their role in achieving the goal of the group. As we saw earlier, this may be either through collective or individual deliberation. For it is through deliberative collective action that individuals settle issues and undertake actions. Surely it is better to look at criminal groups as undertaking collective criminal actions in this fashion; as opposed to using external attributes to explain the actions of criminal groups or the demarcations allowed by academic gang typologies (Gordon 2000). It is also a good idea to distinguish between collective action and collective behaviour: the former being deliberative, in other words purposive, and rationalised in terms of a definite reason and the latter being mere undirected activity. This is helpful since it illustrates how the reasoning of individuals involved in deliberative collective action is an active and dynamic aspect of it. Through a process of deliberation individuals come to perform actions of the sort X performs actions x in accord with their reasons and so are performing an action not a behaviour. When individuals perform collective actions they are doing so in the light of collective goals. I accept that it is possible that collective goals could be undertaken either deliberatively or non-deliberatively but because our focus is upon culpable criminal activity we focus on deliberative instances.

The question is how to explain deliberative collective action? There is distinction being made that holds there is a real difference between collective and individual actions. Moreover, surely some actions are part of sets of actions, individual and/or collective. Furthermore, deliberative collective action has to be set out in terms that *always* relate to a pre-existing, or underlying, collective goal or goals. It is a tricky idea: for instance, if a rational actor when presented with an issue then decides to participate in collective action with others to overcome it, what should their action be in this collective endeavour? I note these things for later.

One thing that is abundantly clear within Criminology is that it cries out for a better explanation of action, especially in relation to group offending cases. At present this is lacking, as is the lack of a thoroughgoing consideration of intentionality and responsibility. This book aims to address this deficit by taking a more philosophical approach. This is not some academic indulgence for criminal justice regularly presents us with group offending cases, including serious offending and joint criminal enterprise cases where there is common agreement that the UK criminal justice systems seems to over-criminalise secondary parties in joint criminal enterprise prosecutions. The effective use of joint criminal enterprise prosecution, moreover, gets more and more shaky where the number of defendants rises (Williams and Clarke 2016, 20). If one thing is certain it is that coming up with a better explanation of the gang, its culture and its ethnography is of no use in accounting for the ascription of culpability in group offending cases or detailing responsibility in specific actions. When put like this it may seem obvious, but you would hardly know it given the lack of attention such issues has had within Criminology. If we try and account for the actions of individuals in group offending cases then better defining gang membership, or the like, fails to account for the *culpability* of individuals in criminal cases where accounting for multiparty agency, and the constituent elements of the individual within it, is an important consideration.

There are several models available to those who wish to tackle, more rigorously, the issue of group offending. In legal theory Kutz has addressed the issue by examining collective intentions. However, he holds to elephantine explanations of instrumentality and participation that load complexity upon complexity and which are neither elegant nor stable (Sanchez Brigado 2010). So we will reject Kutz. Nonetheless we can follow Kutz to the extent that we look at Bratman's work as he did (Kutz 2000). The way forward is to look at two versions of reductive theory, Bratman's and Gilbert's. "(E)very individual acts on the basis of their own *will*, or mental state, and that we can accordingly, say that all collective actions, may, in turn, be *reduced* to a sub-set of individual actions, each enacted by persons in terms of their own will, or mental state … The point to hold onto is that those who hold a reductive theory of collective action view it as the sum of a set of individual actions enacted by a sub-set of wills, or mental states" (Amatrudo 2015a, b, 111). Reductive theory has the obvious benefit that it allows for personal responsibility to be handled in a straightforward fashion. There are non-reductive models available like that of Roth. However, they tend to place considerable limitations upon the agency of individuals by placing too much stress on the collective (Roth 2004). For this reason we shall reject non-reductive models.

Bratman supplies an explanation which is often known as *we*-action theory. *We*-action theory sees shared intentions as the outcome of a set of individual attitudes and relationships. It prioritises the individual over and against the group. Gilbert, on the other hand, maintains that things are better explained in terms of sets of normative transactions that generate interpersonal obligations. Gilbert places more emphasis upon the collective quality of action than Bratman. List and Petit have gone so far as to call Gilbert a non-reductivist (List and Petit 2011). This is far too strong and though she writes of plural subjects she is also clear that these are made up of a prior set of individuals which are, in turn, characterised by their individual, separate and unique wills. Gilbert resists the collectivism of Roth (Gilbert 1999). The task of this chapter is to argue for a more technical, and philosophically savvy, account of group behaviour as opposed to the hackneyed cultural one now dominating within Criminology. In doing this it will hold that criminal activity is merely a sub-category of group behaviour, more generally. Accordingly, both Bratman and Gilbert supply us with robust accounts of collective action applicable to the sorts of issues faced in the criminal justice system around group offending. In using models drawn from accounts of joint commitment and shared intention, that ask important questions about subjects, it is likely that we will get better answers to our queries concerning the nature of multi-agent criminal activity and a more realistic legal framework with which to judge that activity. The work of Bratman and Gilbert can, moreover, give us a sharper lens to better view group offending in socio-legal terms. By insisting upon a technical determination of group offending we will arrive at a safer basis for sentencing in such cases.

However, one should not imagine that reflecting on the work of Bratman and Gilbert is simply of academic interest because there is much in such reflection that could aid the cause of justice and aid the courts, notably in group offending cases. After all, as Pitts has argued, the prosecution of joint enterprise cases in the English courts has not been so much interested in the culpability of parties so much as determining individual bad character (Pitts 2014). This sort of non-technical and associational approach is, moreover, closely correlated with gross instances of racial bias by the police, Criminla Prosecution Service (CPS) and courts (Williams and Clarke 2016). The focus away from the central issues of culpability and justice, as they inform determining specific responsibility for specific acts, in the prosecution of group offending cases, and towards a vaguer sense of association in terms of certain cultural markers is worrying. Indeed Criminology itself gives support to this unhelpful view of group offending with its multiplicity of typologies of persons in groups, gangs. Of course, such typologies have certainly fed into the over-criminalisation of youth, especially black urban youth. The assumptions and the tight, and at best sub-regional, and at worst incredibly localised, snapshot focus of most of the fieldwork that supports such an approach has extrapolated generalised notions of "gangs" which have fed into the mania for joint enterprise prosecutions in the UK. Indeed such an approach has engendered real, though largely unwarranted, fears about such "gangs" being the "enemies of society" (Green and McGourlay 2015). For these reasons the argument shall be set in terms of the principles required to determine joint action, as set out by Bratman and Gilbert. This approach both avoids the obvious moral panic we note in so much academic literature and policing strategies around joint enterprise prosecutions. Surer to think through the technicalities of specific actions than to consider the extraneous, such as clothing, associations around family and friendship, the use of social media, as so forth; all of which are regularly taken into account as evidence of foresight in the prosecution of joint enterprise cases. The task will be to stick tightly to notions of culpability and joint action and away from the mendacious assemblage of: "(G)ang discourse and joint enterprise" (Williams and Clarke 2016).

We-action Theory in Bratman

We-action theory addresses the matter of the goals of individuals by examining the relationship between their intentions in relation to the larger group. The doyen of this approach is Michael Bratman and it is his contention that in order to understand collective action we ought to concentrate upon shared intentions as the starting point for discovering *we*-actions. His work on *we*-actions, and team preferences, appeals to the mechanics involved in the deeper processes of reasoning that underlie collective action, in terms of *shared* intentions. This approach is appealing because it notes that collective actions are nevertheless "reducible to a sub-set of individual, though inter-related, actions" (Amatrudo 2015a, b). The notion is that the actor, the individual unit of personhood and action, is unavoidably the basis of any collective action. This is an important point to note in terms of thinking about the criminal law for it ensures the individual subject may be held personally culpable in group offences. For Bratman the main thrust in understanding shared intentions is to determine whether they are also able to account for team goals. The language of sharing implies a level of intimacy between the parties which is not the case in all conceivable cases of collective action. In simple terms, this is to address the issue of whether it is the case that when a person has an intention to act they simultaneously share a team goal. Moreover, it follows from this that the question arises as to whether the person who shares a team goal shares precisely the *same* intention as the rest of the group. In a formal and technical sense, holding to a goal and sharing an intention are separate activities; a point typically missed in academic Criminology. When we look at an example that Bratman employs then a helpful contrast becomes apparent. Let us think through two scenarios (1) *A* and *B* go on a journey together and (2) *A* and *B* share a journey together. The notion is that the second example is suggestive of a much more interpersonally rich experience than is present in the first example. We take from this that *sharing* a journey, or some other experience, is much stronger than merely collectively participating in it. However, exactly how it is stronger is a more tricky determination. Bratman is not so much concerned with delineating strong and weak notions of goal sharing and accounting for their differential treatment of personal intimacy. Nonetheless, Bratman goes on to set out three sorts of sharing which illustrate this issue. The forms of shared activity he sets out are: (1) a basic commitment to mutual support, (2) a commitment to joint action and (3) a more elaborated notion of "mutual responsiveness" (Bratman 1993). All of these three activities, in their varying ways, centre upon achieving a goal. Bratman is shy of distinguishing in terms of the level of intimacy but instead he uses a technical distinction between JIA (jointly intentional activity) and SCA (shared cooperative activity). He develops this in his article in the *The Philosophical Review*, "Shared cooperative activity." In this piece he sets out the example of two singers who are involved in a duet. The issue he points to is that though their separate actions would bring about a successful duet they fail to support one another in their singing. Bratman shows how if either singer messes up their singing then the other singer does not have the ability to help out. He determines this to be an example of JIA since SCA would entail an additional element, a commitment to mutual support of the other singer. Bratman claims that: "(Any) joint action-type can be loaded with respect to joint intentionality but still not strictly speaking (be), cooperatively loaded ..." (Bratman 1992). We should note here that the question arises whether team goals, on this reasoning, are cooperatively structured or structured in terms of the parties' joint intentionality. Bratman holds that team goals are cooperatively structured. This amounts to saying that those persons who hold to a team goal are more committed than those who simply engage in JIA. Bratman sets out three different sorts of outcomes that can be produced collectively. These are (1) *collectively successful outcomes* in which every actor involved as a party to a joint activity performs a role in order that the joint outcome is realised, (2) *individually successful outcomes* in which an individual actor successfully performs their own contribution to the joint action but other actors do not achieve this and (3) *jointly unsuccessful outcomes* in which the actors neither fulfil to undertake their role and where, consequently, there is no joint outcome successfully achieved. Do note we are using the term "joint" in a neutral fashion because we have no grounds for assuming that joint outcomes unavoidably require the contribution of more than one party. The importance of distinguishing SCA from JIA, for Bratman, is to underscore that those who undertake JIA will value their own individual success ahead of a collectively successful outcome (Bratman 1992). Rather than contest Bratman's claim let us instead take from this that it is possible to delineate actors undertaking JIA from those undertaking SCA: and hold that when we do this we then note that a differential emerges between the values this imposes upon a range of possible intended outcomes. This means that we can hold that possessing team preferences is dependent upon the actors who are party to it being prompted by SCA, rather than JIA.

Collective Action and Intentions in Bratman

The novel contribution Bratman made to the way we think about collective action is in terms of the way he conceived of our *sharing* intentions. He maintained that persons are involved in the collective action, of J-ing, only when they share the identical intention to J in cases of voluntary J. Since it is so important we ought to restate Bratman's formulation in full, before moving on:

> We intend to J if and only if:
>
> 1. (a) I intend that we J and (b) you intend that we J;
> 2. I intend that we J in accordance with and because of 1a, 1b, and meshing sub-plans of 1a and 1b; you intend that we J in accordance with and because of 1a, 1b and meshing sub-plans of 1a and 1b;
> 3. 1 and 2 are common knowledge between us. (Bratman 1993, 106)

It is important to note the technical term that is doing all the work here. The first condition is what philosophers call a *we*-intention and it is central to understanding Bratman's contribution. The second condition he calls the *meshing sub-plans* condition. The main thing to note is that shared intentions may not be reduced to the set of attitudes held by individuals, instead they should be viewed as the appropriate mental attitudes of appropriate individuals

Bratman on Shared Intentions

Let us look a little deeper at Bratman's notion of *J*-ing. Bratman's *we*-intention notes that *A* and *B* share the same intention, *J* being a joint action. However, the issue of just how any individual comes to intend an action that is joint becomes a knotty technical matter as does the issue of control over it (Bratman 1999). Bratman brings in his own form of control, which he terms Condition C. It holds that an individual cannot be said to intend any actions that they *personally* cannot *control* and also *settle*. On the matter of settling, Condition S, Bratman posits that an individual can only intend an action that they *personally* can resolve or settle. This is an important element in Bratman's account and vital to his reductivism. It is nonetheless possible to conceive of *we*-intention conditions that are not bound by the limitations of the C and S constraints that Bratman sets out. In the account Bratman provides, the role of C and S constraints is partly to enable "other-actor conditional mediation" of intentions (Bratman 1999). What he has in mind here is, for example, holding that an individual *X* may intend to facilitate an outcome *o* by performing an action *x* even in a case where *o* requires that some other individual *Y* executes an action *y*; then it is the case that if *X* considers if *o* is produced this rests on the actor who performs *x*. It is the case that when an individual carries out *y* it is conditional upon *X*'s completion of *x*, if *X* knows the individual carrying out *y* is conditional upon *X*'s intention to undertake *x*. In this fashion *X* is able to control and settle the production of *o* simply by having the intention to *x*. Moreover, he argues that it is reasonable to hold that an individual *X* may intend a joint action *J*, when it is believed that the joint action *J* rests, to some degree, on whether *X* holds an intention to do his or her bit, *x*, in the *J*. Bratman is clear on this matter and states:

> When I decide that we paint together, I suppose that my intention that we paint will lead you so to intend as well. Does this mean that, strictly speaking, *you* don't get to settle the matter of our painting or, at least, I don't see you as settling the matter? Well you remain a free actor; it really is a decision that is up to you without which we really will not paint. I predict that, in part as a result of my intention, you will so decide; but that does not

mean that you do not decide. I can predict what I know to be your free decision. I can predict that you will freely, in response to my intention, intend that we paint, and so settle the matter of our painting together. That is why I can now intend that we paint. (Bratman 1999, 1956–7)

Bearing this in mind, let us restate that an outcome o is produced by an individual X performing an action x and an individual Y performing an action y. We could further hold that an individual Y will only perform y if they note X about to undertake x, or where they note X has formed an intention to perform x. Bratman maintains it is correct for X to intend to bring about o by performing an action x, and this controls and settles the matter of the production of o. However, the bigger claim as to whether we can hold that X intends that together X and Y collectively produce o we can only hold, in my view, if X intends that she produces o in terms of her performing x but this is well short of the claim she, X, intends: that they, X and Y collectively, produce o. The major problem here is whether it is right for Bratman to move from his *other*-agent, yet conditionally mediated version of intentionality to a full-on *we*-intentionality model. I am sceptical simply because *we*-intentions are completely different in their form from *other*-agent conditionally mediated intentions. *We*-intentions are characterised in terms of their form by being exemplified by the action not of a single individual but by the action of another individual, or individuals, as well. In order to show this we need to revisit Bratman's "I intend that we J" procedure. To begin with joint actions are necessarily, and obviously, composed of more than one person. Therefore, if an individual X has a behaviour, or set of behaviours, x which she can perform and which, in turn, bring about an action type and another individual Y has a behaviour, or set of behaviours, y that she can perform and which bring about an action type then we can say that the joint action J is composed of an aggregate which may be expressed as $\{Xx, Yy\}$. Moreover, we may make another claim about the composition of joint action that maintains that any joint action J which may be undertaken by X and Y is *always* on a set of further behaviours x and y; so we note that J is always the expression of an aggregate set, $\{Xx, Yy\}$. This is important since it shows how joint action types, that satisfy the compositionality criteria, may always be further broken down to the individual sets of behaviour performed by the participating individuals. This ability to reduce collective behaviour to the actions of its individual members is an important point that has real-world appeal in accounting for culpability when considering joint action in multi-agent criminal cases.

Getting More Technical

It is difficult to sustain the proposition that all joint action types satisfy the compositionality criteria. This is simply because although all joint action types, including cooperatively neutral ones, must fulfil the compositionality criteria in the Bratman plan we note here that because *Jo* is cooperatively neutral from the outside those joint actions that are cooperatively positive, *J+*, appear the same as those joint actions that are not cooperatively positive, *J–*. To the outsider both *J+* and *J–* appear the same, with respect to their external behaviour. This is a big issue for it is not possible for us to allow that *J–*, which is non-cooperative, can appeal to collective goals. *J–*, being non-cooperative, may only ever be sustained by reference to the goals of individuals, X and Y. If we do this then the component activities, x and y, of the parties X and Y, are what establishes *J–* and all that entails is a simple combination of individual action types; and this we establish as $\{Xx, Yy\}$. Since *Jo* is cooperatively neutral it is externally, at least, identical to *Jo*: and the same applies to *J+*, and both are constituted by actions, x and y. We may hold that all joint action types, of the sort we *J*, look precisely the same as joint actions of the sort you do y and I do x. Although Bratman argues that his notion of meshing sub-plans can allow for a common knowledge condition to explain joint actions it appears that his compositionality condition means that ultimately his *we*-condition collapses into circularity (Bratman 1993).

Let us look again at Bratman's *we*-condition formulation that holds: "1. (a) I intend that we *J* and (b) you intend that we *J*." In this case *J* is a cooperatively neutral joint action type which exhibits a compositionality criterion which is identical with the action types of the sort x and y. His second condition holds: "2. I intend that we *J* in accordance with and because of 1a, 1b, and meshing sub-plans of 1a and 1b; you intend that we *J* in accordance with and because of 1a, 1b and meshing sub-plans of

1a and 1b." We could alter this to: *1#* (a) *X* must intend that *X* do *x* and that *Y* do *y* and that *1#* (b) *Y* must intend that *X* do *x* and that *Y* do *y*. This too seems not to be quite up to the job, for how can *X* intend that *Y* undertakes an action or that *Y* intend that *X* undertakes an action? Surely the conditions *C* and *S* ensure constraints on the intentions of individuals and, accordingly, entail rejecting the idea that *X* intends that *Y* undertakes *y* because *X* cannot control (C) or settle (S) the matter of *Y* undertaking *y*. It could be argued that *X* does in fact control (C) or settle (S) to the degree that it could be predicted that *Y* will undertake *y* so long as *X* does *x*. This is what amounts to the foresight condition in UK joint enterprise law (Krebs 2015). Bratman's own view of the settle condition (S) holds that: "Suppose that Diane does not intend to raise the pressure once Abe intends to pump. But Diane is a kind soul and has access to the pressure valve. Recognizing this, Abe might be justifiably confident that if Diane knew that Abe intended to pump water Diane would decide to turn the pressure valve. And he might be confident that if he intended to pump Diane would know it. Given this confidence can Abe decide to pump water? Can he in the relevant sense 'settle' the matter of whether the water is pumped? I think he can, given that he is in a position to predict that Diane will respond appropriately" (Bratman 1999, 1954–5). This is unsatisfactory to my mind, since rather disappointingly, Bratman falls short of showing us Abe settling the issue of whether Diane turns the pressure valve and so all that Abe settles is that the water is pumped. Therefore, all that Abe is able to intend is the outcome of the water pumping. Moreover, it would be wrong to think of the situation in the terms Abe intends, in other words that *they* pump the water together (collectively) through Diane's turning and Abe's pumping. Whilst Abe can surely settle his own pumping of the water he is unable to do the same as regards to their, *collective*, pumping of water. Abe is unable to settle Diane's turning of the valve even though this is a very important consideration. From the outside all we can allow is that Abe intends to pump the water and that it is pumped. The matter that this is all causally related to Diane's intentions too is not so important, although Abe knows that her actions are necessary to the outcome. We can hold that Diane's contribution is just one of the many things that unite Abe's actions with his favoured outcome. It would be misleading to hold that Abe's intention is *their* (his and Diane's) pumping of water as this implies that he can settle both his pumping and, crucially, Diane's turning. If we held that Abe could settle Diane's turning that would be tantamount to holding that she is not a sovereign person; indeed it is not possible.

We might contend that an individual, X, could bring about an outcome o that rests both on their undertaking x and another individual, Y, undertaking an action y. This is obviously not the same as contending that X intends that collectively, *they*, generate o by means of the one doing y and the other undertaking x. It is safer to argue that X has in mind to produce o by means of their doing x, but in the knowledge that their undertaking of x will facilitate Y doing x; and thereby the outcome o will be achieved. It is not possible, however, to maintain that X can ever intend that they bring about o as that would entail X to intend y and conversely that Y intends x. This is unsatisfactory as we have seen already that X can neither control (C) nor settle (S) Y's carrying out of x. So, in the end, we have to hold that Bratman's notion of the *we*-intention is flawed simply because he never furnishes us with reasons for accepting *we*-intention grounds without simultaneously *asserting* that individuals involved in joint action possess *we*-intentions. We cannot allow such an assertion to be sustained as it seems to breach the sort of reasonable conditions necessary to maintain a rational basis to *individual* intentionality.

The account Bratman provides us is one that tends to account for collective action in reductive terms; that is to say in terms of *individual* actors. These *individual* actors deliberate and act in terms of their own individual states, though these might also be interdependent. This is clear but it only really allows a full account of the *individual* actor and his, or her, *individual* actions. In the Bratman account the only serious difference between examples of individual and collective action is that in the case of collective action there would appear to be a dependence upon the individual and upon others to enact a given action rather than their enacting it alone. It is though, a *reliance*, not a straightforward matter that can be both controlled and settled, which we would require for a robust account of collective action. In Bratman's account it is the case that X's intention that both X and Y undertake J is only something that X can control if he is certain that Y too will share, and act on, the same intention to J. The problem, as we have already noted, is that X's intention remains what we technically call *other-actor enabled*, in other words it only ever refers to their personal action. This means that the content of such an explanation cannot truly be said to be referring to *collective* action at all. Likewise, if Bratman holds that the intention refers to Y's actions too then this clearly breaches the important own action condition that holds that individuals may not intend the action of other individuals. It may though, we can concede, be possible to intend some outcome o that is collectively enacted.

Plural Subjects in Gilbert's Account

Margaret Gilbert follows in the footsteps of Searle in that, like him, she understands that the defining feature of a joint action is invariably correlated to its elemental internal composition (Searle 1997). Her elaboration of joint action states that the important feature of any internal composition lies in it having a *shared* aspect to it. Her notion of shared intention is not given as an aspect of the particular form of intention an individual may possess: instead Gilbert conceives of it in terms of relationships, in other words in regards to the obligations and interpersonal obligations that spring from any shared intention. In this regard she elaborates a very sociological understanding of joint intention. What is more her work exhibits a much richer sense of the collective nature of collective action than does Bratman. This has led Sheehy to argue that her writings show the requirement for an ontological commitment by actors to any joint commitment (Sheehy 2006).

Ethics of Joint Commitment

In Gilbert's account we note that we can only fully understand social phenomenon by first understanding the underlying composition of the beliefs, groups and intentions that give rise to it (Gilbert 1992). The notion that Gilbert works is straightforward; it merely asserts that it is possible for individuals to think, and act, as a collective and that they do this much of the time. This is what Sheehy had in mind when he noted

Gilbert's ontological commitment. She holds that there are "plural subjects of intention" and that, advancing a version of holism, we simply cannot explain joint action by restricting actions and beliefs and intentions to those of individual actors (Gilbert 1992). This is a very important element in her work though holism has been roundly criticised by scholars who note that it often tends to underplay the role of individual agency in group action (Harding 2007). Gilbert, I think, avoids this trap. She sets out a technical formula for interpreting plural subjects: "*Schema S*. For the relevant psychological predicate '*X*' and persons *P1* and *P2*, *P1* and *P2* may truly say: 'We *X* with respect to *P1* and *P2* if and only if *P1* and *P2* are *jointly committed* to *X*-ing as a body'" (Gilbert 2000, 19). In outlining *Schema S* she sets out not just the form of joint commitment but the form for all of her views on plural subjects. The idea is that all forms of commitment have two basic categories, joint commitments and personal commitments, and, furthermore, that all commitments are reducible to these two categories. Gilbert notes how any individual can generate personal commitments as they like with no constraint upon that endeavour. This means that individuals may also rescind those commitments at any time. Gilbert writes how "… if and only if he is the sole author of a commitment and has the authority unilaterally to rescind it" (Gilbert 2000, 21). This is in contradistinction to the altogether more problematic incidents of joint commitment where more than one person is involved and where the commitment is jointly undertaken. We note that such joint commitments are an aggregation of the concomitant commitments of those parties to it. There is a technical point to note also and it is that Gilbert rejects the idea of joint commitments being composite in nature (Gilbert 2000, 53). In Gilbert's scheme joint commitment is defined in terms of it being created by the parties *together* and so the only way to annul such a commitment would be for parties, similarly, together to determine their wills to annul it (Gilbert 2000, 21). What this means in a practical sense is that if any one party to a commitment breaches their commitment the commitment is not breached, in terms of the original joint commitment; instead Gilbert asks us to view it as a violation. This is because she determines that the original commitment has real status in its own terms. In *Living Together* she explains that "the parties to a joint commitment are tied to one another" (Gilbert 1996, 295). This illustrates how Gilbert understands the situation in terms of all of the parties needing to mutually annul joint commitments as no single party has the power to do this. The important point she is expressing here is that the entire enterprise of individuals coming to mutual agreements necessarily generates coterminous *interpersonal* entitlements and obligations; which is also interesting sociologically. Her notion that mutual agreements are necessarily implied in any joint commitment is her major contribution in this area (Gilbert 2000, 26).

Gilbert on Plural Subjects

By going back to her *Schema S* it is possible for us to set out, more fully, Gilbert's concept of the plural subject and to say something meaningful about its relationship with the notion of intentionality. She sets out three key features that relate to shared intentions, which she relates back to the notion of a plural subject, in order to explain it. She does this using the example of two persons who decide to go on a walk (i.e. a walk *together*). So initially she states that two persons decide (i.e. have the intention) to go on a walk together. The question then arises as to what happens should one walker decide to end the walk. For Gilbert it is clear that the person who decides to give up on the walk is deviating from the original shared intention to go on a walk *together*. If this happens, and one party unilaterally ends the walk, Gilbert holds that they deserve a rebuke since the other party has what she terms "(a) special standing …by virtue of the (original) shared intention" (Gilbert 2000, 16). When situations like this arise in the context of shared intention several things follow, for Gilbert:

(1) In the Gilbert formulation it is clear that the parties involved are obliged to always act in terms of the shared intention and that such obligations are necessarily directed at the realisation of the shared intention.

(2) All shared intentions produce concomitant entitlements, and rights, upon all the actors involved in relation to the achievement of the preferred outcome.

(3) Should any party to a shared intention act counter to it then it follows that all the other parties to it may rebuke them. (Gilbert 2000, 17)

If we consider these three elements together we note that they form Gilbert's obligation criteria. Furthermore, that this obligation criteria binds parties to the shared intention that they make (Gilbert 1999). However, what of the case, for example, when one of the walkers gives up due to tiredness? Gilbert still holds here that there can be no unilateral termination of the walk and argues that the person giving up would have to gain permission from the other party, or parties, since in her scheme all the parties must agree (Gilbert 2000, 170). This is not to state that it is not possible, only that it needs all parties to agree any annulment. Gilbert's account of shared intentions rests upon this *permission criterion* and it underpins her criterion for deciding the sufficiency of the agreement. She also advances a *compatibility criterion* to determine the sufficiency of the situation which maintains that the intentions of all parties must correspond and not merely coincide with each other (Gilbert 2000, 17). We note how her idea of shared intention is rigorous, and conceptual, and holds that shared intentions necessarily entail recognition of the obligations and rights associated with any given joint commitment.

The Role of Joint Commitment and Obligation in Gilbert

It is a defining feature of Gilbert's work that shared intentions and joint commitments are intrinsically tied to one another. Moreover, that the existence of joint commitment implies a supporting set of relationships in terms of interpersonal entitlements and obligations between all the individuals involved. Gilbert's particular version of joint commitment has a set of characteristics associated with it. Joint commitments are always given, or rather directed, in terms of obligations to particular parties. In this fashion, parties are obligated to one another in terms of a matrix of corresponding entitlements and rights (Gilbert 2000, 104). Moreover, these obligations that are expressed through joint commitment are not set out in either moral or prudential terms (Gilbert 1992, 163). This is because, she argues, that morality and prudence are insufficient in terms of animating parties in joint commitments. This I do not follow and believe morality could animate parties; as Sheehy has noted (Sheehy 2006, 70). It also complicates matters if joint commitment is to be conceived of outside of morality or prudence. What Gilbert does is to advance her theory in *associational* terms and, in her terms, as *political*. In *On Social Facts* she notes how they are associational in terms of their association with *particular* joint commitments; in other words that they are not generalised (Gilbert 1992, 411). She states that they are *political* in a limited sense because such an association always entails a concomitant underlying network of mutual respect and support (Gilbert 2000, 103). It is only when there is a breach that the obligations of joint commitment may be lifted from the other party, or parties (Gilbert 2000, 60). She holds that obligations of joint commitment are always unconditional in the sense that they are not dependent on other conditions (Gilbert 1996, 352). The big claim that Gilbert makes is that joint commitment always provides the parties with a sufficient motive to act (Gilbert 1996, 288; Gilbert 2000, 243). In expressing the obligations of joint commitment in the way she does Gilbert sets out a clear, sociologically-savvy, model that provides a rigorous and importantly, interpersonally normative, structure by which to interpret action.

X-ing as a Body and *Schema S*

It is necessary to return to Gilbert's *Schema S* formulation in order to set out, more fully, her work on social action. She notes that:

> *Schema S.* For the relevant psychological predicate '*X*' and persons *P1* and *P2, P1* and *P2* may truly say 'We X with respect to *P1* and *P2* if and only if *P1* and *P2* are *jointly committed* to *X*-ing as a body'. (Gilbert 2000, 19)

As Tuomela has already noted it is the underlying commitment to shared intention that Gilbert is dealing with in *Schema S* (Tuomela 2005). Nonetheless, the notion of "*X*-ing as a body" needs some elaboration, especially as it is quite a subtle psychological idea and in *Sociality and Responsibility* it is the thing that grounds Gilbert's notion of the collective nature of action. At its most straightforward "*X*-ing as a body" relies on the idea that the collective, made up of two or more persons, may act "as a body"; in other words, although it is plural it nonetheless acts as though it is a single body (Gilbert 1996, 348). We might hold that there is a deal of circularity in this reasoning and note that, upon this reasoning, if we were accounting for the idea of a shared intention by employing *Schema S* then we would understand that employing "*X*-ing as a body" is problematic since "*X*-ing as a body" implies joint intention, the phenomenon it seeks to determine. This need not be fatal for Gilbert but it certainly necessitates a better, in the sense of a fuller, account of "*X*-ing as a body." It requires a further psychological predicate to note intention in order to better account for the notion of "intending as a body" along the lines Gilbert employs in *Sociality and Responsibility* which states that: "Persons *P1* and *P2* have a shared intention to do *A* if and only if they are jointly committed to 'intending as a body' to do *A*" (Gilbert 2000, 22). If we employ the example Gilbert uses of Ruth and Lil who share an intention to paint a kitchen together then, argues Gilbert, this amounts to Ruth and Lil, jointly, making a commitment to paint the kitchen, "as a body." That is to say, in practical terms, their joint commitment affords grounds that satisfy *their* shared intention. Gilbert posits: "(Both) has reason to act, make plans, and so on, in conformity to the joint commitment" (Gilbert 2000, 24). The point being that this rationale facilitates them having sufficient reasons to act exclusively in terms of the joint commitment they made. In this way, Gilbert provides Ruth and Lil grounds to fulfil their shared intention by means of having an assemblage of thought and action that relates precisely to their shared intention of painting the kitchen together. In short, a shared intention is supported by a matrix of actions and thoughts which make it possible. In other words, Gilbert shows that the idea of "intending as a body" can be understood as the sum of the actions, plans and thoughts that make it possible at all. Therefore, if we employ the interpretation that I suggest we can maintain that "intending as a body" explains precisely what it means for Ruth and Lil, acting together, to share an intention, in this case to paint the kitchen, but which will hold for any version of "*X*-ing as a body." This seems fairly straightforward as a practical rationale.

Before we make some more progress let us nail down a few remaining issues relating to "*X*-ing as a body." One important point to note is that

"*X*-ing as a body" rests upon a set of actions, plans and thoughts that specifies the content of any given joint commitment. As we saw previously, Gilbert notes how the joint commitment sets out the reasons for the parties to it to act in accord with their joint commitment. In this way "intending as a body" sets out precisely what it means to act in regard to *their* understanding of shared intention. So we can concur that "intending as a body" sets out elegantly and exactly what it entails to act in accord with Gilbert's understanding of joint intention. Though it is necessary to recall that there is explanatory force in using the psychological predicate "to intend" as that sets out the actions, plans and thoughts that establish "intending as a body" in the first place. After all, Gilbert claims that the actions, plans and thoughts that establish "intending as a body," and in the case of Ruth and Lil this relates to painting the kitchen, does not require their personal intentions to paint at all (Gilbert 1996, 349). The technical term for this sort of reasoning is *disjunctive* since the assemblage of actions, plans and thought are separated from Ruth and Lil's *individual* needs to fulfil their shared intention of painting the kitchen together. If we think of it another way, there must be in place a set of attitudes before Ruth and Lil's painting of the kitchen but, of course, each can only ever undertake a sub-set of the necessary attitudes required. Or put another way, each does her part in "intending as a body." In Gilbert's work on plural subjects, and the capacity of those plural subjects to hold collective beliefs, rests on these two technical formulations: in other words "intending as a body" and "*X*-ing as a body." Gilbert maintains that:

> The behaviour that results from collective belief is driven by the concept of belief and the concept of *X*-ing as a body. It is as if the participants ask themselves 'what do I need to do to make it the case – as best I can – that I and these others together believe that *p* as a body?' … the answer given by our everyday understanding for the simple interpersonal case is that, among other things, in reasoning together we say things that entail *p* rather than not-*p*, we do not deny *p* without preamble, and so on … We attempt as best we can to make it true that the body we constitute relates to *p* the way any individual who believes that *p* relates to *p*. (Gilbert 1996, 356–357)

Gilbert notes in *Sociality and Responsibility*, that if individuals believe themselves to be sharing an intention then we may infer actions that both reflect and support that belief (Gilbert 2000, 50–70). This is an enormous claim but it does open things up. Her work is plausible because it is so sociologically rich; it is not simply located within technical analytical reasoning. Gilbert's whole idea of "as a body" when applied to shared intentions itself rests on the *a priori* existence of collective beliefs. Her work illustrates how there must necessarily be a background of actions and thoughts before shared attitudes can be developed. The notion of "X-ing as a body," as set out in *Schema S* illustrates this. In *Sociality and Responsibility* she sets out the proper relationship between "We X" to "X-ing as a body" in terms of shared intentionality. Gilbert offers us a clear-cut model that steers clear of circularity. When we concentrate upon shared intention we can note a distinction between shared intention and the notion of "intending as a body." We note how *shared intention* is a much stronger term because underlying it is the presumption both of "intending as a body" and joint commitment. Whereas "intending as a body," though it notes the bundle of actions and thoughts entailed in shared intention, is not adequate to the task of joint commitment. Now with this in mind, if we think of "X-ing as a body" along these lines then *Schema S* becomes useful, not circular at all.

On this summation "X-ing as a body" opens up the whole topic of plural subject evaluation, especially with regard to more individualistic rationales. The way to understand "X-ing as a body" is as something that is invariably comprised of a collection of acts and thoughts which are individual. As a result of this *collection* of acts and thoughts, members of a group come to possess a different type of subjectivity; they are plural subjects of X, this being the upshot of jointly committing with others and also to others, to X as a body. This we saw as the case with Ruth and Lil when their shared intention to undertake something, painting a kitchen, was seen to be the aggregate of their individual attitudes. We noted too that this formulation does not breach Gilbert's holistic nature of the plural subject test because, on my understanding of her writing, the shared intention is rooted in a deeper joint intention. This is the case because the underlying notion of joint commitment is itself a holistic one (Gilbert 1992, 13). She argues in *Sociality and Responsibility* that "… the core concept of plural subject theory is this holistic concept of joint commit-ment" (Gilbert 2000, 3). My preferred reading saves "*X*-ing as a body" from the innate circularity of the *Schema S* formulation and it also adds a psychological richness to the understanding of shared attitudes that is compelling.

The Unresolved Problem of Joint Action/ Commitment

The final matter to address in regard to Gilbert's work is to ask whether it is useful in assisting us to think more clearly about the relationship between joint action and joint commitment. Her writing on joint action is always tied to a prior understanding of joint action (Gilbert 2000, 3–5). Gilbert makes a distinction between joint action and coordinated behaviour by pointing out how joint action necessarily entails joint com-mitment to it by those involved in it whereas coordinated behaviour does not. There is no more to her distinction than that and, moreover, it is the basis of all her work on shared agency. The notion she advances in regard to joint commitment exhibits a couple of technical elements that are noteworthy: (1) it is what is called *primitive*, that is to say, it cannot be reduced to a more simplified form and (2) it creates obligations between those involved in it (Gilbert 1992). We may pull back from going all the way along with Gilbert here in her conception of joint commitment. For example, there are issues in terming joint commitment as *primitive* since it does not altogether clear up the problem to turn to some other notion to explain the main issue, that of joint action. In terms of obligations being generated by joint commitment, this has the danger of slipping into circularity and that joint action and joint commitment are presented as somehow codependent upon on one another. In holding that joint commitment generates obligations between the parties to it, one might argue this only makes appeal to the concept it was meant to be explain-ing. The larger problem is surely to do with the nature of what counts as joint and, indeed, how we distinguish between joint action and coordi-nated behaviour because the line between them seems fairly blurred.

Moreover, we need to resolve this matter of joint commitment in Gilbert since it is the heart of her whole understanding, not only of this technical question but in terms of her conception of the whole social world. It is fair to say that Gilbert tends to use joint action to resolve the matter of shared intention, if not conflate them (Gilbert 2000, 40–70). I find this not entirely successful but with a few technical reservations I feel Gilbert has nonetheless set out some cogent points in relation to shared intention. She usefully utilises a sociological viewpoint in her speculation, notably in terms of the nature of interpersonal obligations we might associate with shared intention. She is right to uphold a sociological approach. Although we may dissent from the particular technical form she outlines in regard to shared intention and obligation; she is surely correct to assert the associational, and moral, nature of obligations and the weaker sense of the individual they presume (Amatrudo 2015a, b).

Going to New York Together

If we turn to Bratman's 1993 essay "Shared Intention" we note some interesting features associated with his constructivist ideas about collective action (Bratman 1993). Bratman posits a few prerequisites for his notion of shared intentionality. There is only collective action where there are two or more persons, where it is the case that the *we*-intention condition is satisfied and where all the parties concerned are intent upon the same joint action with meshing sub-plans, and this is known by all the parties involved. Bratman's most well-known, and most controversial, example is his "Going to New York Together." In this he illustrates how through the process of intending that the sub-plans of all the parties to the collective action concerned mesh and that the parties, individually, also intend that they are enabled by the other member, or members, of the group. This amounts to a mutual respect of individual agency. This reasoning allowed Bratman to rule out what are known as Mafia examples where, although both parties intend to go to New York, one of the parties is the subject of duress or where agency is bypassed, as would be the case if one of the parties were taken there in the boot of a car. We see how Bratman's meshing sub-plans usefully outlaw Mafia examples on the grounds that they do not respect the other party's individual agency, indeed they do the opposite. What Bratman wants is a model of collective action that prohibits coercion or failure to respect the agency of others. Bratman's model of collective action is founded upon meshing sub-plans, which are known between the parties, and mutual respect.

Although he sets out a clear position on collective action, Bratman's model has several issues related to *we*-intention associated with it. One issue is that his other agent, conditional mediation, cannot account for the reasons why a person comes to intend that some group of persons undertakes a collective action. He notes himself that a given intention, which rests upon another person acting in a particular way, cannot tell us why they intend a joint action (Bratman 1999). One might conclude that it is reasonable to think that there can be a form of intention which posits that those individuals undertaking collective action are focused not upon their own individual action but upon some collective action involving others. This is though quite tricky because it would appear to suggest that an individual intention focused upon a group enacting a collective action also infers that this necessarily imposes constraints upon others, in order that the collective action is performed. Surely, it is far safer to argue that individuals all possess separate intentions that the group enacts, some outcome. Moreover, we might argue that different actors who, separately, consent to their intentions are in some way constrained by the particular goal that the group holds. This would appear to be the favoured way to understand Bratman's notion of the *we*-intention condition. It is a practical and rigorous approach to the problem of collective action. It will rest on the understanding that individuals who undertake collective action, and deliberation, in regard to a collective goal are nonetheless constrained by their outcome intentions and that this is facilitated by a notion meshing sub-plans that are conditional upon a collective action. In terms of this meshing sub-plan condition, we note in Bratman's example of "Going to New York Together" that there the individual's plans do mesh because the ultimate outcomes are a function of the two persons acting collectively. However, there is a major discrepancy between, on the one hand, one person putting another person in the boot of a car to get to New York and, on the other hand, the two just taking a train to

New York together: one being a breach of the collective intention provision that Bratman stipulates and the other being the realisation of it.

However, we might imagine that if two persons did in fact share the same sub-set of plans would it always hold that just because they mesh that entails both persons holding the same collective intention? By way of example, what if one preferred to get the bus to New York and the other wanted to take the train? In such a case we could say that though they are both cooperating, in getting to New York, they nonetheless are involved in other reasoning too. Moreover, this is a very common scenario especially in games playing and sport. We could set the matter aside and hold that the form of transport is incidental and that what really counts is that the collective outcome is satisfied; and that is possible in a variety of ways. Maybe we ought to acknowledge the multitude of ways of getting to New York and that the form of travel is less important than the "going to New York together" so long as the key elements hold, in other words that there is a common agreement, "going to New York together", that constrains their deliberations and that the parties concerned are involved in collective reasoning. We do not always need to invoke Bratman's notion of meshing sub-plans because it is merely an aspect of the way we appreciate outcomes as flowing from the actions of persons. In terms of the condition that collective action is the outcome of individual agency, all this requires is that individual choices are respected and that the individual agency of parties is also respected. As to Bratman's notion of common knowledge this needs to be thought of as a belief of common knowledge, as opposed to common knowledge *per se*. If all the actors involved *believe* that the condition concerning common knowledge is satisfied, this is sufficient. If the actors concerned believe the common knowledge condition is satisfied then we can sustain the claim that the parties share a common goal. What Bratman wants to achieve is to maintain a theory of collective action that can contain a plethora of possible varieties of "going to New York together" and at the same time rule out Mafia cases as bona fide examples of collective action. This he achieves and, following my reading of Bratman's work, we note how to distinguish between legitimate cases of collective action, in this case of "going to New York together," and Mafia cases, which are usefully excluded on clear technical grounds.

Why Advocate for a More Technical Approach to Multi-Agent Criminal Cases?

There is a clarity and sense of practicality in the work of Bratman and Gilbert that is undoubtedly applicable to both the academic treatment of multi-agent criminal activity and the prosecution of joint enterprise criminal cases. The reductive theory we find in Bratman and Gilbert, though not entirely unproblematic, is a good basis for the study of joint agency. The main benefit is that rather than proceed on the basis of vague notions, such as foresight, they begin their theorising with much more profound issues relating to collective agency that are at the root of joint enterprise and the key notions of action, commitment and shared intention. By focusing upon these technical issues that are neutral, as between individuals of different sorts, they usefully avoid matters of prior affiliation, class and race. At the outset we noted the report *Dangerous Associations: joint enterprise, gangs and racism* that clearly demonstrated how talk of "gangs" played into an underlying racial prejudice as shown by the policing and prosecutorial strategies around joint enterprise; and which in practice reinforced such stereotypes (Williams and Clarke 2016; Young 2014). The point we need to bear in mind is simply that joint criminal action is just another form of joint action, albeit a proscribed one, and therefore it is a good candidate to follow the reductive theory we find in Bratman and Gilbert. After all, surely criminal action belongs to a broader range of action and so can be understood in such terms. Bratman reminds us that individuals compose any collective action. It follows then that any joint action, J, is always an aggregate set of individual behaviours, $\{Xx, Yy\}$. This means that the compositionality facet of joint action means that it is always conceivable that it may be reduced to the actions of individuals. Gilbert's model is far more complex, but it nonetheless has a much enhanced *collective* aspect. Gilbert's work allows us to conceive of the "plural subject" in which case persons intend, or believe, or have in mind a goal and so can think collectively (Gilbert 1992). Gilbert's plural subject is not composite in the way that Bratman suggests; it rather suggests that the parties to any commitment create, *together*, a joint commitment which if any individual breaches they violate

(Gilbert 2000, 21, 53). In Gilbert we note that the parties to any joint commitment are mutually committed to it and, furthermore, it binds them as though they are tied to each other as a result of it (Gilbert 1996, 295). Her work stresses a mutuality of relationships, between the actors, which exhibits coterminous *interpersonal* entitlements and obligations. On my understanding of her idea of "*X*-ing as a body" we note a rich psychological sense to her work that is allied to a sociological awareness of the nature of shared intention. Both Bratman and Gilbert allow us to focus upon what really matters in multi-agent criminal cases, joint action. Their focus is always upon action and what happened. Neither, Bratman or Gilbert, are concerned with wider cultural or phenomenological matters. In multi-agent criminal cases this is a safer way to approach such cases. Of course, there can be joint (criminal) enterprise but the work of Bratman and Gilbert encourages us to prove it through investigating the commitments and intentions that make it up. We should never presume it by noting the cultural associations of dress, linguistic code or even "gang" affiliation (Williams and Clarke 2016, 18).

Bibliography

Amatrudo, A. (2010). Being Lucky and Being Deserving and Distribution. *Heythrop Journal, 51*(1), 658–669.

Amatrudo, A. (2015a). Unheimlichkeit: Alienated and Integrated Identities and Criminal Existence(s). *Law, Jurisprudence, Governance and Existential Indeterminacy: Onati Socio-Legal Series, 5*(3), 969–981.

Amatrudo, A. (2015b). Individuals and Groups of Individuals Breaking Laws. In D. Crewe & R. Lippens (Eds.), *What is Criminology About?* (pp. 105–122). Abingdon: Routledge.

Amatrudo, A. (2016). Applying Analytical Reasoning to Clarify Intention and Responsibility in Joint Enterprise Cases. *The Politics and Jurisprudence of Group Offending: Onati Socio-Legal Series, 6*(4), 920–936.

Bratman, M. (1992). Shared Cooperative Activity. *The Philosophical Review, 101*(2), 327–341.

Bratman, M. (1993). Shared Intention. *Ethics, 104*(1), 97–113.

Bratman, M. (1999). *Faces of Intention: Selected Essays on Intention and Agency*. Cambridge: Cambridge University Press.

Gilbert, M. (1992). *On Social Facts*. Princeton: Princeton University Press.

Gilbert, M. (1996). *Living Together: Rationality, Sociality and Obligation*. Lanham: Rowman and Littlefield.

Gilbert, M. (1999). Obligation and Joint Commitment. *Utilitas, 11*(2), 143–163.

Gilbert, M. (2000). *Sociality and Responsibility: New Essays in Plural Subject Theory*. Lanham: Rowman and Littlefield.

Gordon, R. (2000). Criminal Business Organisations, Street Gangs and 'Wanna Be' Groups: A Vancouver Perspective. *Canadian Journal of Criminology and Criminal Justice, 42*(1), 39–60.

Green, A., & McGourlay, C. (2015). The Wolf Packs in Our Midst and Other Products of Joint Enterprise Prosecutions. *The Journal of Criminal Law, 79*(4), 280–297.

Harding, C. (2007). *Criminal Enterprise: Individuals, Organisations and Criminal Responsibility*. Cullompton: Willan Press.

Krebs, B. (2015). Mens Rea in Joint Enterprise; A Role for Endorsement? *Cambridge Law Journal, 74*(30), 480–504.

Kutz, C. (2000). *Complicity: Ethics and Law for a Collective Age*. Cambridge: Cambridge University Press.

List, C., & Petit, P. (2011). *Group Agency: The Possibility, Design and Status of Corporate Agents*. Oxford: OUP.

Pitts, J. (2014). Who Dunnit? Gangs, Joint Enterprise, Bad Character and Duress. *Youth and Policy, 113*(1), 48–59.

Roth, A. (2004). Shared Agency and Contralateral Commitments. *The Philosophical Review, 113*(3), 359–410.

Sanchez-Brigado, R. E. (2010). *Groups, Rules and Legal Practice*. London: Springer.

Searle, J. (1997). Responses to the Critics of the Construction of Social Reality. *Philosophy and Phenomenological Research, 57*(2), 449–458.

Sheehy, P. (2006). *The Reality of Social Groups*. Chippenham: Ashgate.

Tuomela, R. (2005). We-Intentions Revisted. *Philosophical Studies, 125*(3), 327–369.

Williams, P., & Clarke, B. (2016). *Dangerous Associations: Joint Enterprise, Gangs and Racism*. London: Centre for Crime and Justice Studies.

Young, L. (2014). *The Young Review: Improving Outcomes for Young Black And/ Or Muslim Men in the Criminal Justice System*. London: Ministry of Justice.

2

Collective Actions and Goals

This chapter is not so much concerned with group offending or criminal actions, *per se*. It is nonetheless integral to the book in that it details issues that are new to criminological theory. The issues of decision making, goal setting and intentionality are surely very much in play when we think through such matters as joint criminal enterprise and determining culpability in a criminal case: they ought to be factored in when considering multi-agent criminal activity generally.

Developing a *Practical* Model of Collective and Deliberated Goals

We saw how thinking about collective action can usefully open up criminological thinking in the first chapter of this technical section. In this second chapter I want to set out a view of collective action that focuses on the notion that collective action *necessarily* entails that all the parties to it are promoting the *same* collective goal. This is not the only view and some philosophers, like Susan Hurley, have argued that collective action does not require collective goals at all (Hurley 1989). I am

© The Author(s) 2018
A. Amatrudo, *Criminal Actions and Social Situations*,
https://doi.org/10.1057/978-1-137-45731-8_2

not attempting a critique of Hurley, and others, merely advancing a defendable position that has real-world implications, not least within the criminal justice system. At the outset it is right to state the major issue under dispute: what do we mean when we discuss collective goals? My view is that there can only be either collectively *exclusive* goals or collectively *inclusive* ones. A collectively exclusive view would need to uphold that there is no necessary requirement to make explicit reference to the actions of individual members of the group in question (Searle 1980). *A* and *B* may hold different collective goals. *A*'s collective goal refer to his part of the robbery as part of the gang's collective endeavour and *B* might refer to his part in the robbery as his contribution to the collective endeavour. A collectively inclusive view, on the other hand, would need to hold that the two robbers "rob together" and hold that both *A* and *B* hold a collective goal to rob and therefore that the collective goal being expressed should be *collectively* inclusive (Bratman 1999). What I wish to establish is that goals are, in a very important way, indistinguishable from intentions. In other words, goals refer to an actor's action in precisely the same fashion as intentions do; leaving aside whether they are individual or collective in nature. Then we might think of goals as referring to the actions of actors in as much as they curb both the considerations and the actions of those actors in question. However, either means of understanding collective goals (i.e. whether they are inclusive or exclusive) has its own technical problems. If collective goals are understood as inclusive that would seem to jeopardise the key constraint upon intentionality which is that actors only intend to both perform an action they are in sole control of and intend an outcome that they have control over. Indeed Michael Bratman makes this claim throughout his seminal *Faces of intention* (1999). Of course, those constraints would differ as to whether we are discussing action or an outcome intention; but in both cases the constraint would always be in terms of what is technically termed the *own-action constraint*. All intentions must be constrained in terms of the ability of any actor to intend their own (i.e. personal) actions. Yet how can that be compatible with a notion of collectively inclusive goals? If *A* has the collective goal of robbing with *B* then it looks like *A* is also intending *B*'s action and that would appear to infringe the own-action requirement. If we utilise a collectively exclusive approach to collective goals then one struggles to locate where the collective aspect is. If A's collective goal did not affect another's actions then it is hard to say how that the goal is collective at all. Moreover, if A intends to rob, as part of a gang of robbers, why would we think of that as a narrowly individual goal and not as a collective goal held by all in the gang? If we held that A robbed as a fulfilment of his part in the collective goal then we would not have a way to analyse collective goals and their internal composition. Moreover, there lurks another matter to address when utilising a collectively exclusive approach to collective goals. If we are to treat goals as being collectively exclusive then it is inexact to claim that the actors involved share a common goal collectively. Instead, it is far better to state that each actor has a collective goal which contains within it their personal contribution to the collective goal. It seems that if we were to think of collective goals as being somehow shared between the members of the collective then that seems to jeopardise a sensible analysis (Sheehy 2006). Since, how could it be determined with any degree of precision what the nature of the collective goal that is being followed is? My position follows on from Bratman's with some practical reservations. I will show how all the parties to a collective action also have intentions that form the basis of their collective action, or actions. Therefore, I will have to explain the matter of whether these individual intentions refer to the collective action in an exclusive or inclusive manner. My account will be collectively inclusive as the criminal justice system requires individual accountability at the end of the day; and this is my view. The danger is always in terms of violating what is technically termed the *own*-action requirement. This *own*-action requirement places various restrictions on the content of any actor's intentions and any model or theory would need to bear that in mind. *Own*-actions need to both adhere to a collective goal whilst also allowing those same actions to be understood as individual. I will establish exactly what we mean when we speak of goals and say how such goals are associated with intentions, inevitably so. The main thrust will be to show how collective goals are better comprehended as outcome intentions. In this way, it will be more apparent how actors hold collective goals and how such goals inform the deliberation of actors. Moreover, it will establish that collective goals do not violate the *own*-action requirement, which may have been a concern. Importantly, the underlying position defended will hold that whilst a collective goal advances coordination between actors it can never fully ensure there will always be a satisfactory level of coordination between them. Nonetheless, this line of argument will be useful for criminologists, and lawyers, asking serious questions about both the responsibility for *individual* action and the relationship between actors.

Goals and Intentions: Building on Bratman

Michael Bratman instructed us that there are two aspects to intentionality. On the one hand, intentions can be understood as instigating deliberation so therefore *limiting* our future actions. On the other hand, intentions can be understood as the outcome of deliberations, and therefore are all about bringing about some future outcome. It is a matter of perspective and where one locates intentions in time, as it were. Bratman noted how these two readings are obviously at odds (Bratman 1987). What we need to do is to make a clear division between goals and intentions. We shall do that primarily by asserting that intentions possess far more by way of what are termed "consistency criteria" than goals do (Bratman 1984). This bifurcation of goals and intentions is important. Bratman considers how an actor may possess two contradictory goals, and yet, also be aware of that inconsistency (Bratman 1984, 375–405). In his technical example, he uses a computer game and considers the case of a player trying to hit two targets and where an actor would have the aim of hitting a target but where hitting either one does not entail the aim of hitting the other. It is a complex example, granted. However, what Bratman wants us to do is to realise that intentions are not synonymous with goals and how therefore it is not inconsistent, or irrational, to hold the goal of hitting both target one and target two; though it would be if the actor held the goal of hitting both. Bratman is not precisely clear what a goal is here, only that they do not require the strict consistency criteria attached to them that intentions do. Consistency matters very much since it specifies how *intentions* help us determine the permissibility of a range of possible options. What Bratman does is to focuses upon the decision-making process. *Goals*, on the other hand, are not subject do not filter an actor's decisions and are not bound by any consistency criteria we might want to apply in the same fashion. This seemingly small distinction comes into play when we model deliberation formally; although we may wish to approach goals and intentions in a similar fashion because not only will that aid simplification but usefully concedes that both are indeed comparable terms since they both serve as inducements to attitudes and constrain deliberation. However, whilst intentions serve as negative constraints on an actor's deliberation, as an intention to *x* rules out deliberation of any action at odds with performing *x*, goals do not actually impose any such rigid constraints upon an actor's deliberation. If we return to Bratman's example of the computer game we note how a goal to hit a particular target does not actually exclude actions since there are other targets. This distinction between goals and intentions is arguably better set in such negative and positive terms. A goal requires a *positive* constraint upon an actor's deliberation to the extent that it suggests an actor should deliberate on what actions will bring about the goal. Goals specify actions actors *should* take. Intentions, on the other hand, impose *negative* constraints in terms of suggesting what actions an actor *should not* take. Intentions, I argue, entail both sorts of constraints, negative and positive ones, whereas goals only seem to entail positive constraints.

I think that we can think of goals and intentions similarly, despite the differences that seem to imply different mental states. Goals can be understood as a restricted form of an intention wherein an actor deliberates solely in terms of the narrow goal. In this way, goals are a restricted form of intention which operates by promoting a particular outcome that ignore all other mental states an actor may have. We may think in terms of goals as being localised. In Bratman's example, we might object that the actor in question is deliberating on a plurality of goals simultaneously, not independently; though it is implausible, in phenomenological terms, since we rarely, if ever, deliberate consecutively about very much. So, the objection to Bratman seems overly formal. We ought also to think, arguably, about outcomes being simultaneous too. In Bratman's example, there might be an objection that runs along the lines of the actor deliberating upon a common outcome and not two outcomes. It is neither irrational to *hold* two different goals, which are incompatible, simultaneously: nor is it irrational for an actor to act in accord with two incompatible goals simultaneously. The whole point of Bratman's example is to demonstrate how it can be the case that acting upon two incompatible goals may deliver another higher goal. It is, though, irrational for an actor to deliberate upon two incompatible goals simultaneously where the deliberation is un-separated. I think that much is clear.

My position is to think of different processes of deliberation as being technically corresponding, or coterminous, if their different goal outcomes, within the deliberation, are viewed as concurrent. That is, in circumstances where two, or more, goal outcomes are considered a single goal. In this way, the actor's deliberation can be understood as simply a process focused upon one goal. It would be irrational to imagine an actor seriously deliberating upon contradictory goals. This interpretation, of actors being unavoidably coterminous deliberators, does represent something of a challenge to Bratman's view. It is my view that rational actors do not engage in coterminous deliberation about incompatible goals. Moreover, we can, in any case, think of deliberation as being simultaneous but not necessarily also non-extensive, as in the Bratman example. An actor holding a goal either knows, or does not, what actions they intend to bring about a goal outcome. Where it is the case that the actor knows, then they need only perform their intended action. In a case where an actor does not know what action they need to perform to bring about the goal then they must deliberate on the goals separately to consider the range of possible options.

Let us imagine that an actor X has two goals, producing $q1$ and $q2$. However, these two goals are noted as incompatible. The actor understands that he cannot produce $q1$ and $q2$ but he has not *specifically* deliberated upon the action required to enable $q1$, and the same holds for $q2$. If our actor X was following my line then he, or she, might well be deliberating upon producing both $q1$ and $q2$, a joint outcome, which we can represent as $\{q1 \leftrightarrow q2\}$, which is an outcome that contains both $q1$ and $q2$ *together*. The actor's deliberation is concerned with which out of a broader range of actions a goal is promoted that is likely to result in $\{q1 \leftrightarrow q2\}$ (Bratman 1993). However, we should note here that as $q1$ and $q2$ are incompatible, or conflicting, then we might say that this is what is technically termed an *empty set*; in other words, that there is no situation possible whereby both of these two outcomes could be produced simultaneously (Salsa 2016). The bigger point is that what this amounts to is to assert that none of the options available can result in a successful joint goal outcome and that the set of joint goals cannot be created by the actor whatever he chooses to do. In usual examples of deliberation, an actor may choose from a range of options in terms of which one best produces his favoured outcome *q1*; which entails deliberation upon only the goal outcome that supports *q1*. The same is true regarding *q2*. If the actor's deliberations about goals *q1* and *q2* are concurrent (i.e. existing at the same time) but coterminous (i.e. having the same spatial or temporal scope or boundaries) that would allow him or her to deliberate about actions in support of *q1*, without regard to deliberating about actions in support of *q2*. Of course, this reasoning is precisely what he should do to increase his chances of hitting target one. He should undertake actions that promote hitting target one and that is equally true in the case of target two (in the Bratman example). An actor may deliberate upon two incompatible goals simultaneously but *only* if the deliberations are separate since the actor *X* needs to evaluate the utility of a range of actions necessary to facilitate the incompatible goal outcomes distinctly. Actors may simultaneously deliberate upon two incompatible goals and be deliberating separately, and this cannot be said to be irrational. This reasoning is readily applicable to the example Bratman uses. I think we need to concede here that, in maintaining the incompatible goals simultaneously held by actors, this may be understood as two separate matters, each with its own discrete sets of intentions. However, we may admit that nonetheless the deliberations, though separate, may affect or constrain in the other case. It is, at least, reasonable to hold this position.

My suggestion is that we think of goals as intentions but of a very limited sort. In which case, we can state that any goal that is directed at an outcome *q* is equal to the intention to facilitate *q* in the context of a deliberation. If actors have a goal to facilitate *q* deliberately, in the sense that they have an intention to facilitate *o*, then we can hold that both the goal and the intention necessarily restrict any deliberation in an equivalent fashion. So, actors that intend to facilitate *o* deliberate in terms of having a goal to facilitate *q*. If we return to the Bratman example, we have a choice of options. It is possible to think of the video game scenario by delineating the two forms of deliberation; in which case, the actor deliberates about hitting target one discretely from deliberating upon target two. Alternatively, we can think of the actor's intention/goal as about hitting one of the targets in terms of it not specifying either target one or target two. The crucial thing to note here is that irrespective of how we decide to conceive of the deliberation the actor is involved in, we can still represent the constraints that he confronts in his deliberation. It derives from goals or from intentions: but these two variables (goals and intentions) can be treated synonymously.

Goals and Rational Decision Making

It is necessary to underpin any view of decision making by saying something about my idea of human rationality. We may not know with any certainty what the possession of a goal will have upon an actor's deliberation unless we are sure whether it is a rational goal or an irrational goal that seems reasonable. This is important since we are only interested in *rational* actors. My view, and it is important for matters of culpability and guilt, is that when there is an assumption of *intentional-rationality*, which may be in the form of *goal-rationality*, then there is no need to ask whether, or not, the formation of any goal is rational or not. Instead we need only concern ourselves with the issue of an actor's choices being rational since we have established that goals have a rational status. This large assumption, that *intentional-rationality* holds, gives us two important features. (1) That the deliberations of actors must be consistent with any given set of intentions since *intentional-rationality* holds that actors may possess jointly possible intentions. This entails that it is possible for an actor to conduct all of their intended outcomes. (2) That the outcome of any deliberation must harmonise with an actor's intentions. In other words, an actor's deliberation must have real determining force. Moreover, in cases where an actor's deliberations are non-determining, then these too must be compatible with his earlier intentions. We hold that this version of *intentional-rationality* is a form of means and ends rationality. An actor's goals should be compatible with their ends. In the best way of fulfilling their ends, the actor is moved by matters of significance. However, the matter of how to decide upon decision-making problems in a system of *intentional-rationality* is tricky and here, given our general approach, we have two basic options, MPDMP or SPDMP (i.e. multi-party or single party decision making problems) to choose from.

Single-party Decision-making Problems

The definition of a single-party decision-making problem (SPDMP) is simply any decision-making matter that is understood by the actor as being one in which he, or she, is the sole participant affecting the eventual outcome. This does not amount, however, to the claim that he is the only person whose actions are *relevant* to bringing about a given outcome. If we think of an example to illustrate this, it might be street robbery. A robber A deliberates about who they should rob. However, street robbery entails not just A deciding to rob but for another actor B to be robbed. Yet the situation is not just set in terms of A and B, the robber and the victim. Robber A settles the matter once he, or she, decides to undertake the robbery. However, B's behaviour (i.e. decision making) is also an element in the robbery, though A does not really consider it. In A's view any behaviour (decision making) that B undertakes is because of the choice (to rob). Whatever B does is irrelevant to A's view that he will commit the robbery. This is the key point in SPDMP: the deliberating actor understands that his, or her, choice *alone* determines the matter. As we think of intentions as being like goals, the rational actor who maintains a goal should always choose actions that advance that goal by taking full advantage of preferences in line with their intentions.

Multi-party Decision-making Problems

In contrast to SPDMP, multi-party decision-making problems (MPDMP) have the deliberating actor as only one part of the decision-making process and the outcome is considered always to be the outcome of more than a single choice or any single actor's choice. We can think of MPDMP as akin to the reasoning in game theory where decision making needs to be resolved (List and Petit 2011, 14). The major issue at stake here is what game theorists refer to as *equilibrium*. A useful working definition of *equilibrium* would hold that no single actor could possibly bring about a situation that would better suit himself, or herself, by altering their choice when the choices of others are left unaltered. This has recently been discussed, in considerable detail, in a recent essay "Imperfect choice or imperfect attention: understanding strategic thinking in private information games" (Brøces et al. 2014). This concept has been most championed, most often, within economic theory in terms of the Pareto Principle (Fleurbaev 2015). The complicating factor is intentionality since actors must choose such actions as they imagine will both bring about an outcome they want and which coheres with their intentions more generally. The issue here is that every actor in a MPDMP necessarily must both hold to their own personal intentions yet also come by, or intuit, beliefs concerning the intentions of other actors and to do this they must assume a very high degree of rationality on the part of other actors. If we hold that all the actors are rational then, and only then, can we model the decision-making problems of all the actors in the MPDMP in terms of the overall compatibility of the intentional states of all the actors concerned. This is what is termed *intention compatibility*. This has been explored most in terms of consumer behaviour and buying activity (Jayasingh and Eze 2015). For our purposes, we need not pursue it mathematically save to say it can result in some very complex forms of modelling, which is why it is used more in economic modelling (Varian 1987).

Delineating Intentions: Actions and Outcomes

It is the Finnish philosopher Raimo Tuomela who drew our attention to the centrality of delineating action intentions from outcomes intentions to understand how collective reasoning is achievable at all (Tuomela 2005). What we must establish is how we can simultaneously account for action, intentions and the *deliberation* entailed in collective cases. This is a complex thing, for every actor deliberating there are corresponding actions and beyond that there is also a relationship between actions and outcomes to be established. Should we conceive of actors as deliberating about actions or should we think of actors as deliberating about the outcomes they wish to produce? Moreover, actors may only perform actions; they cannot normally bring about outcomes on their own. The SPDMP model is straightforward as it offers a deterministic structure for actions and outcomes. In SPDMP cases it is not very important if intentions are thought of as either action intentions or outcome intentions. Action intentions restrict choices; so do outcome intentions. For all actions, we may construct an equivalent outcome intention, and for any outcome intention we may construct a range of actions that cohere (Wahl 2016). Things are much more complex in a MPDMP where we must necessarily think of action intentions in a completely different way from outcome intentions, since no single actor may bring about an outcome alone. Moreover, we might add that there is no necessary relationship between an actor's action and any outcome; and the same holds for an actor holding any given intention. MPDMP reasoning is about intentions and actions, but not in terms of establishing a specific outcome. All an actor may do is to intend a range of outcomes which are a set of outcomes that other actors are available to undertake. Action intentions intended by an actor may be thought of in terms of X intending an action x where the intention entails all outcomes (x, xn) so that xn is the possible range of actions for all the other actors to execute in the MPDMP. If an actor's intention to cooperate does not entail another's action then it seems to be that an actor's intentions are only to perform an action and not crucially focused on bringing about a particular outcome. In MPDMPs we seem to have both intentions that are determinant and other which are non-determinant. We can state that determinant intentions are about exclusively determining actions for a given actor to undertake whereas non-determinant intentions do not have this exclusive sense. An actor with determinant intentions is, to some extent, giving up their own capacity to choose the outcome that they are partly producing. They are giving other actors in the MPDMP the decision-making problem and handing it over to them for their choice. Determinant intentions are unconditional since they do not rest on the actions of actors in any given MPDMP decision problem: and any outcome produced in the MPDMP, by the other actors, still needs to be compatible with the actor's own intention, otherwise his, or her, intention would be irrational. This is because an actor in this situation is stating that he, or she, is content with whatever decision outcome the other actors choose to bring about. If this were not the case, then an action intention would never have been originally formed.

When we think of non-determinant intentions things are far different. When actors form non-determinant intentions in a MPDMP they are stating that certain actions would be irrational for them to perform. In other words, any outcomes which spring from such actions would also be unjustified on those grounds. Here we note that action intentions could be outcome intentions. Simply put, when an actor has an action intention he or she also has an outcome intention to bring about all outcomes that flow from his or her undertaking that intended action. However, this is not the case with outcome intentions which cannot be conflated with action intentions. If we look at arrangements in an MPDMP, we understand that an outcome needs the input of more than one actor. In the MPDMP, the holding of an outcome intention entails an actor having an intention to produce a definite outcome while an actor with an action intention only has to undertake a particular action. We note here that that an actor may control an action intention and he or she may have confidence in it. The outcome intention is more complex and certainty is much less sure; this is because he or she cannot be certain of what the other actors in the MPDMP will enact as their contribution to the outcome. The actor in the MPDMP may have faith in their contribution to the outcome, but they cannot intend an outcome of which they do not have overall control. An important point to note here is that of autonomy; all actors in the MPDMP choose separately, necessarily so. The main thing to keep hold of is that although actors do not have direct control, within a MPDMP, over the actions and decision making of others, nonetheless an individual does indeed have some *limited* element of control through their actions. An individual in a MPDMP may only hold that their action intentions contribute, not determine, an outcome. This is because of the power of the own-action requirement which could be said to undermine the formation of a truly collective action.

The Problems of Action Intentionality

I have detailed how, when modelling intentions and outcomes, intentions may be understood as goals. What we need to establish is the matter of collective goals. For a range of actions to be termed collective action there must be a prior reason stage (Gilbert 1999). This collective reasoning is always focused on a goal, a collective goal, which the actors involved want to generate between themselves. We need to ask profound questions about the fundamental nature of collective goals. Simply put, we hold that individual goals structure an individual actor's deliberation and collective goals similarly structure the deliberation of the collective (i.e. group of individuals). We hold that collectives are best understood as reducible to individuals and their singular properties. In terms of collective goals, we hold that collective goals are best understood as the outcome of the goal-adapted behaviour of the actors that constitute the collective; though the goal-adapted behaviour of individuals must be understood in terms of the goal-adapted behaviour of the collective. Any actor deliberating in terms of the collective necessarily deliberates towards a goal that is structured in terms of the collective.

It can be pointed out that there are examples of where reference is made to collective goals without making mention of the behaviour of the actors that make up the collective. In other cases, it can be shown that only some members of the collective undertook an action. This kind of issue arises mainly in relation to very large-scale collectives with a political, or sociological, dimension like a city, a region or a state. In terms of these grand-scale collectives, one may well talk of collective goals although a large proportion of the group may neither have made any contribution to the collective goal nor even be aware of it. An example of this might be fighting a war, when a whole country may be said to have the collective goal of winning, although most of the citizens make no real contribution to that end. In such grand-scale cases, we are not doing anything technical and there is no specificity. These grand-scale cases are better understood in terms of social identification and social action, as Gilbert argued throughout *Sociality and Responsibility* (Gilbert 2000). These grand-scale scenarios we will not explore. In the fullest sense, collective goals need to consist of the actions of all members of the collective. It is still possible to hold that some actors may not undertake such actions that are necessary for the collective goal to come about, but who nonetheless have their actions, choices and deliberations organised in accord with the collective goal. This explains how looking at actions alone does not assist us in fully accounting for collective goals. This is because collective goals need to reference the actual behaviour of the collective, i.e. the behaviour of all its members. Whereas this is not the case with action intentions, which do not reference the actions of all members of the collective: for any actor who undertakes an action in a MPDMP, it does not matter what others do as he or she fulfils their action intention. It may be argued that since the action is rooted in the MPDMP that some reference is made to the action undertaken by other actors in the collective. Moreover, the actor will certainly hold beliefs about the intended outcome which can only be enacted by the agency of others in the MPDMP. This would not help us since it is easy to show that this line of reasoning is not so much taken with intentions but with beliefs. The collective goal needs to *structure* the deliberations of all members of the collective and the impact of any collective goal upon the deliberation of actors will always vary from person to person. In the case of action intentions, it is hard to see how one arrives at a single collective goal that structures the deliberation of all the members of the collective if we understand things narrowly in terms of action intentions. How could one delineate a case where all the actors hold action intentions which amount to a collective goal and the case where all the actors hold action intentions which do not amount to a collective goal? We may not distinguish between these cases simply because an actor possesses an action intention and thereby intends some *individual* action (Searle 1980).

Moving to Conditional Intentions

One may imagine that these problems could be placated by invoking intentions that incorporate *conditional* action, in other words employing conditional action intentions. In which case, we could hold that a range of action intentions may, together, form a collective goal where those action intentions are held to be *conditional* on the other actors performing their role, as has been reasoned in prisoner's dilemma scenarios (List and Petit 2011; Xiao and Unfeather 2012). In most examples, however, it is not easy to explain conditional intentions in terms of the rational deliberations undertaken by the actors involved. However, thinking about conditional intentions allows us to reason that an actor can come to a decision concerning his or her actions in an uneven, or asymmetric, situation. We may think of it simply as: (1) an actor may form an action intention, and then it follows that (2) another actor responds with a corresponding action intention. This is not possible where actors deliberate simultaneously since we hold that conditional intentions are part of the actors' deliberations. In this way actors would form an action intention straightforwardly *or* the necessary conditional intentions would have been already met and so are understood as straightforward action intentions. The issue for collective action is surely that if we are to think about deliberating actors acting simultaneously then this would seem unhelpful since actors tend to form their intentions and to act in response to one another. If asymmetry is the way to go then there is the matter of starting collective goals and seeing them in terms of action intentions that are *conditional*. Conditional action intentions fall short of fully explaining collective goals. Moreover, as collective goals are tangible (in the sense of being clear, substantial and quantifiable) they may be said to structure the deliberations of actors within the collective. There is a requirement to ensure the conditional intentions are tangible, which implies that actors come to form their own tangible action intentions. The asymmetry between actors involved in conditional actions *always* remains. This is not ideal since it implies that someone, an individual actor, should become the instigator of every single collective action which is implausible in every case; though plausible in some. If we look at Roth's work, we note he intimates that there must be an instigator in every case of collective action; that is, there is always a leader who gets the collective action up and running (Roth 2003). However, he fights shy of stating this as he understands that actors have their own conditional intentions and in his essay *Practical Inter-subjectivity* he is dubious of the possibility that conditional intentions can explain collective action (Roth 2004, 359–410). One thing Roth seems clear on, however, is that there will be asymmetrical relationships in any case of collective action; though he is sceptical of them arising with respect to conditional intentions.

Margaret Gilbert offers us another, more nuanced, account of conditional intentions. Her methodology employs a dual-stage procedure when theorising how intentions are formed with regard to collective action. Initially, she argues that actors must signify their readiness to jointly commit to being party to a plural subject and that only then may they proceed to form action intentions that are rooted in their *constituted* nature as a plural subject. In this way Gilbert allows for asymmetry and, using her plural subject reasoning, shows us how the important thing is not the sequence of how actors jointly commit to being party to a plural subject, but that they do it at all. When actors jointly commit to being party to a plural subject then it naturally follows that they also take on all the necessary commitments that entails (Gilbert 2006, 3–17). This model looks promising at first glance. My reservation is that whilst it appears quite neat to tidy up some issues it still cannot discriminate between authentic cooperation and strategic game playing. Let us examine the case in terms of the prisoner's dilemma (PD) model. If actors, *A* and *B*, are in a PD situation they both signify their conditional action intentions along the lines that Gilbert sets out and, without making a commitment, they nonetheless imply a willingness to engage in cooperation dependent on the other actors expressing a commitment cooperate. Note that such expressions of this type of conditional willingness fall short of being in any way binding and neither can they be considered binding on other actors expressing a conditional willingness. These *expressions* are not intentions, nor can they be said technically to be conditional intentions. They are merely expressions and only amount, at best, to a willingness to construct some intention; but an intention that rests upon certain other elements being fulfilled. Moreover, this expression to construct an intention may itself be undertaken for simple strategic reasons though also, admittedly, to enable other actors to undertake some cooperative intention.

If *A* says they will cooperate and *B* says the same the issue is: ought they then cooperate? *A* may very well be more certain that *B* has an intention to cooperate but, crucially, *B*'s intentionality does not restrict *A*'s ability to deliberate. So, does *A* really have an intention to cooperate in this scenario? The rationale for cooperation is not really proven. The expression of conditional willingness we note in terms of forming an intention to cooperate falls short an intention. It fails to restrain *A*. For *A* to possess constraints on his or her deliberation he or she would require a personal intention of his or her own. Therefore, the way to think about Gilbert's dual-stage procedure around conditional intentions is simply in terms of it furnishing us with a model of beliefs for the actors involved. When actors state their willingness to conditionally construct an action intention to cooperate what we have, in Gilbert's dual-stage account, is *A* and *B* endeavouring to inform each other about the state of their beliefs about what they are doing. Actor *A* desires that actor *B* will think she is going to cooperate, and vice versa. Ideally this could all be totally sincere and *A* and *B* may go on to form an intention to cooperate. However, the situation may be less candid and the reasoning of the parties, actor *A* and actor *B*, may be strategic and there is no guarantee in this model that either party will do as they say. Gilbert does not give us strong enough grounds here. The problem of setting a clear basis for conditional intentions that accommodate collective goals is problematic. The problem being that there is an asymmetry when we try to model conditional action intentions; and that complicates how one might account for conditional intentions, in terms of the necessary constraint specified. Therefore, when we think of modelling collective goals then arguably outcome intentions are a more fruitful way forward.

Collective Goals and Outcome Intentions

To begin with it is important to note that outcome intentions can furnish grounds for collective goals whereas action intentions fail to do so. The activity of cooperative reasoning diverges from individual reason since it always fixes upon *team* goals, not individual goals. We have already noted how individual goals constrain individual actors in their deliberations to the extent that deliberating actors act in accord with the goal outcome. It seems obvious, but we note here that individual goals also constrain individual actors. Goals imply a restraint on action to the extent that they restrict the range of considerations and actions that an actor may have and yet still be rationally in pursuit of a goal. Individual goals may be also understood as action intentions. In terms of the PD if A has the goal of cooperation this is the same as their having the intention outcomes in which A is involved in cooperation (List and Petit 2011, 107–108). This is what game theorists call encoded information regarding. However, it does not encode for B's actions because the intention is necessarily compatible with any possible action that B may undertake. This is not the case with collective goals since they relay information concerning the entire membership of the group (Guilfoos and Duus Pape 2016). They are about collective deliberation first and foremost. The task being to understand what that actually means *technically* in terms of how collective goal setting works both for a group, as a group, and for individual members of a group. The usefulness in alighting upon outcome intentions is that they can explain collective goals because they refer to the actions of all the actors in the group. That is, if we think of outcome intentions allowing an actor to enable a range of outcomes. This means that all outcomes reference those actions that enable the intended outcome. If we think in terms of the PD we may note that a key outcome intention would be that of reciprocal cooperation between the parties; and that is surely an outcome that refers to the actions of all the actors concerned, as the outcome necessitates that all actors cooperate to produce the intended outcome (Taylor 1987). Individual goals focus the deliberations of actors whilst referencing those actions in terms of his intentional agency, whereas collective goals focus the deliberations of the group whilst referencing the actions of the group. In both instances, the conditions are fulfilled by outcome intentions. Outcome intentions refer to the action of all actors in the group as the outcome is facilitated by all the individual contributions of the actors in the group for it to be enabled. These outcome intentions structure an actor's deliberations but only insofar as they are part of the group. In an MPDMP all collective action is the outcome of the actor being a party to it. It follows that outcome intentions are the held by all parties to the MPDMP. In a PD game, we can reason straightforwardly that if we hold that the parties wish to advance an outcome intention of reciprocal cooperation then all parties need to hold that outcome intention. It is the outcome intention which focuses the deliberations of those concerned and which make it rational for them to cooperate at all. This is not the same with collective outcomes which do not necessarily structure the actor's deliberations, for example one can imagine a case where actors hold the same outcome intention but in which one engages in cooperation but the other does not. So, we can say that outcome intentions signify a collective goal by signifying only those outcomes that the group seeks to enact. We must think of outcomes as a variety of actions undertaken by a set of actors (group) and by signifying the outcomes that the actors rationally enact. Secondarily, outcome intentions refer to the individual actions of those in the group. We can hold that collective goals in terms of the process of deliberation can be seen best in terms of outcome intentions. The real problem is simply according for how any model of collective goals can be congruent with the necessity of maintaining, also, the own-action condition criteria.

Own-action Conditions

In all that has been said, it is a supposition that outcome intentions are not liable to infringe their relationship with own-action conditions; and, such as we have seen thus far, any constraints are negatively formulated, in other words they do not really concern mental states. What I mean here is that if we theorised in terms of positive constraints then if an actor had the intention to undertake some action this would impose a positive constraint upon them. If the actor failed to undertake such an action then they would have not fulfilled the normative condition they placed on their intention. This is not the case where things are negatively configured, in which case the negative constraints on the actor require that he or she undertake the contents of their mental state. What negative constraints do is to impose a prohibition upon undertaking actions that do not satisfy the contents of his or her mental state. Therefore, in the case where an actor has an intention to undertake an action then that is understood negatively. In which case, his or her intention will necessitate him or her acting upon the norm and *foregoing* all actions that do not promote the action. It is clear so far that we have really been advancing a line of reasoning that models intentions in terms of their having negative constraints. In the form that I advance them, intentions are understood primarily in terms of their *constraining* deliberation, and this is a *negative* constraint. Negative constraints are congruent with constraining the actions of other actors and positive constraints are not. This is because positive constraints are always structured, technically, in terms of undertaking a given action. If understood positively then actors need to undertake their part but also the action components of the other parties to the collective. This, of course, threatens the actor's own-action conditionality. This problem arises in the work of Michael Bratman where his writing on collective intentions, understood in terms of *positive* intentionality, leads him to suggest that actors also come to intend the actions of others, as I noted in Chap. 1 (Bratman 1999, 1954–5). The deployment of negative constraints allows that there is no necessity, positively, to mandate actors to undertake any action. Instead negative constraints constrain actors from undertaking any action that is not compatible with the intended outcome. An actor's intention to undertake an action requires them to levy negative constraints to *not* undertake actions that are not compatible with his or her actions. Such constraints are pertinent to an actor but only to the extent that he, or she, deliberates over actions that are incompatible with this model. We note how these negative constraints have no impact whatsoever upon an actor's other deliberations. If we move to collective goals, we further note that when an actor has a collective goal that a collective, C, should enact an outcome q then he, or she, surely understands that the *collective* goal constrains his or her deliberations. They must hold, on this basis, that any action undertaken which is incompatible with producing q is, in this model, irrational. It is simply absurd to hold that an actor could ever accept constraints on the deliberations of other actors who are in the C.

This is at the heart of the difference between individual and collective goals. If a person holds a collective goal of facilitating q then he, or she, as a part of the group C understands that the collective goal of facilitating q is being facilitated by the agency of the whole collective, above all else. It is the group that has the determining agency not the individual. The actor understands that there is a rationally determined constraint upon the deliberations of all parties to C. An actor's deliberation is only ever influenced by the constraints that relate solely to his or her own-action. Otherwise there are no constraints upon his or her deliberations and certainly none deriving from the constraints upon other parties to C; since those do not impact upon the choices he or she makes. Let us say that the constraints that derive from collective goals do certainly affect other parties to C, but that these are of little consequence, although they do help us discriminate between different sorts of goals, namely collective and individual ones. In the case of collective goals, actors note how constraints do affect other parties to C and in the case of individual goals how they do not. We have already noted how actors with individual intentions are not held to constrain other actors since the intentions they hold impose no constraint over them. The case is different with collective goals simply because their function is quite different. Collective goals are all about the deliberation of groups and not of individuals. Accordingly, they refer to the deliberations of all the actors in C not simply individuals within it. This is an important point. The dilemma is set in terms of explaining how such collective goals may structure the deliberations of a collective yet be said to be possessed by individual actors too. We noted earlier how collective goals may constrain the deliberation of a collective when they are held by all its members. In a case where all members of C have the same collective goal, it follows that the deliberations of C will be effectively constrained in a way that produces the necessary intended outcome. However, since collective goals are possessed by individual actors it is not required that all the parties to C hold the exact same goal for it to be a collective goal. Actors may have false beliefs about the other members of the group. They might deliberate on a collective goal in the belief that another party holds the same collective goal, when they may well be deliberating upon an individual goal. What I am drawing attention to here is that an actor's deliberation upon a collective goal cannot constrain the deliberations of the rest of the group and therefore it is surely inadequate as the basis of a collective goal. After all, this is what a collective goal should do. For an actor to hold a collective goal, all that is necessary is that the actor must have a belief about the other actors in the group, namely that they too hold, deliberate and act in accordance with the collective goal. It could also be pointed out here that any actor who doubts that other members of C share the collective goal cannot themselves truly, in the sense of authentically, hold a collective goal since that is a *sine qua non* in terms of collective goals. The collective goal must be underpinned by a belief condition. Goals are collective when constraints affect the deliberations, and the actions, of a group of actors and individuals. In either case, goals are always conceived of in terms of outcomes. The essential difference in goals is conceived of in terms of whose actions they are focused on constraining.

Positive Constraints and Negative Constraints

To restate my view: collective goals can be congruent with own-action conditionality as they relate to negative constraints. Moreover, as collective goals refer to the actors in C they do not breach own-action criteria since they are understood in terms of negative constraints. In other words, all the parties to C are only constrained in their actions in terms of those actions that breach the collective goal. Actors in C are not expected to undertake the actions of other actors since they are not understood in terms of positive constraints on their actions. This dichotomy of constraints, positive and negative, is the key point to note here. In Chap. 1 I noted how Michael Bratman's elaboration of collective action in terms of *we*-intentions appears to have some issues in terms of it specifying both sorts of constraints, in other words positive and negative constraints. We hold instead that Bratman's notion makes it very difficult to sustain a straightforward procession from deliberating to actual action. We understand negative constraints as *privative* in that they only specify what is not to be done; some other account must be furnished for positive actions. This being the case, we note that intentions tend to be invoked by theorists of action simply because they can furnish both positive and negative constraints on actors. In this model, having an intention to undertake an action q entails an actor constrained not to undertake any action that would contradict q and also to act positively towards q. In my model, having an intention, or a goal, to undertake q only entails not undertaking an action which is at odds with his or her undertaking q. In the model, I advocate that positive constraints are focused on the decision-making element, the *deliberation*. If an actor deliberates they thereby create a positive constraint and the problem is centred on the way to resolve the issue of what actions to undertake. When an actor faces a problem about what actions to perform then that in, and of, itself acknowledges the deliberation issue and also entails a positive constraint in terms of his or her undertaking the q suggested, in terms of her intentions. The decision-making problem is the element we look to for positive constraints. It is noteworthy here that we make explicit that the positive constraint that follows from the decision-making problem is not made in terms of the actual content of the actor's intentional state. In resolving the decision-making problem, actors have positive constraints in undertaking actions that are underpinned by reasons but that is not to argue that they have positive constraints of undertaking whatever the content of their intentions is. Any actor who possesses a collective goal that refers to the other parties to the C does not also have any positive constraints relating to undertaking the action of the other actors. Instead the only positive constraint they have is to undertake actions that are underpinned by reason. Unlike in Bratman's model, this version of collective goals holds that actors only have positive constraints regarding their own *personal* actions (Bratman 1992). There is an issue relating to the determination of whether an intention is held rationally, or not, in the case of collective goals. Moreover, we would need to bear in mind whether, or not, an individual actor is reasonable in his or her deliberations upon a given collective goal and ask whether C is reasonable, as a collective, in holding a given collective goal.

Returning to Collective Goals

If an actor rationally holds an intention it makes no real difference whether the goal is individual, or collective, in character. The main thing is surely that he or she must *believe* that his or her actions will come to satisfy the goal. In the case of the actor holding a collective intention this means that the circumstances are in place, externally, for his or her intention to be settled. There is a need to make the underlying key acceptance conditions more readily understood in terms of their role in facilitating collective action and move to note the relationship between key acceptance conditions and collective action. The essential thing to note about these key acceptance conditions is that they set out an actor's beliefs concerning the configuration of the MPDMP. Moreover, the beliefs in question must be commonly held beliefs, in other words the actor must hold that all the other actors in the MPDMP possess the same belief. The most basic of these commonly possessed beliefs is in common agency. As we established earlier, for an actor to possess a collective goal he or she must hold beliefs about the other actors in the MPDMP and they, in turn, must *collectively* reason that others hold the same beliefs. The essential point here is not to state that all the actors in the MPDMP necessarily hold, individually and collectively, a belief about the other actors. We are stating instead that the actors in the MPDMP believe that there is a common belief in the MPDMP. The rational basis for the collective goal lies in the *common belief*. There are certainly outstanding technical issues concerning the constitutive account of the collective, but these are not a consideration when deciding upon the rationality of actors, in terms of their possession of collective goals. As well as the matter of the common agency condition, an actor must also fulfil the common goal condition for him or her to possess a collective goal that is rationally come by. All a common goal condition requires is that all the actors involved must hold that the collective goal is well-known among all the parties to the MPDMP. The issue is not that the goal is actually held by all the parties in the MPDMP, but that all the parties *believe* that the goal is commonly held. The main thing we note is that there are rational grounds for possessing, and acting upon, a collective goal. Finally, we note a common predicament condition which amounts to thinking about the actors in the MPDMP as all believing that all the other actors confront the same decision problem and that it is also common knowledge between all of them. Of course, collective action can happen even without these key acceptance conditions in place, or even when they are breached. However, if key acceptance conditions are absent then how can any rational actor possess a collective belief and yet fail to also satisfy key acceptance conditions? Where an actor knows that another actor possesses different beliefs about what actions constitute a MPDMP then, surely, they cannot be certain of the other actor holding the collective goal and that this will then result in the desired outcome. What is more, if an actor persists in holding a collective goal in the light of the divergence between his or her view and another's, that would *ipso facto* be irrational; although one can imagine circumstances, even in this situation, where actors nonetheless take part in collective action.

The important point about collective action is that all the constraints that it throws up are held by *all* the actors that are party to it. As one actor does their part of the collective action he, or she, is sure the other parties are too. This is simply because the actor understands that the other actors are similarly constrained through the mechanism of the collective goal in terms of their personal, in other words individual, deliberations and actions. However, we must admit that actors may not be able to know the precise parameters of the collective goal. There may an imprecise understanding of how individual actions contribute, precisely, to the collective goal and as to what exactly that collective goal consists of in any detail. These things mean that attributing blame and *responsibility* for the success of a collective action in case of an iniquitous action (e.g. crime) can be an inexact enterprise. This ambiguity entails, I suggest, that we adopt the notion of a core belief in modelling these situations to account for actors involved in collective action *believing* that all the other actors hold the same collective goal. This seems a reasonable and real-world approach.

If we think in terms of rationality then we might reason when it may be rational (i.e. reasonable) to possess a collective goal. Here, it seems, the way forward is not so different to the case of the individual goal. Typically, collectives are understood as akin to individuals – if you like super-individuals – at least for the purposes of understanding the rationality, or otherwise, of goals (Amatrudo 2016). If we stick to examples where actors hold *legitimate* beliefs about the nature of collectives they belong to, then we note how, as with individuals, that collective intention can be thought of either in terms of the goals being preference rational, which implies an ability to measure those preferences, or in terms of their being intention rational (Sugden 2000). It remains the case that there will always be a coordination problem (Colman 2003). Whatever actors do to harmonise their activities, success can never automatically flow from simply having a collective intention in common; however good the communication is between them. The goal may never be realised in practice (i.e. in the real-world).

Conclusion

We end our technical discussion by asking questions about the nature and extent of common goals. Common goals can be understood as individual ones to the extent that actors reason them *individually*, though their end is known by the other actors in the group. This employment of individual reasoning means that actors can rationally predict the reasoning and actions of other parties. The main point to note is that actors deliberating in terms of common goals necessarily deliberate individually and their actions are restricted by their holding a common goal. Every actor reasons in terms of goals that restrict their range of possible actions, and this holds for every other party to the collective goal. It is plausible for all the actors involved to hold a belief that every other actor holds the same collective goal. For any given actor, there is more certainty about his or her reasoning than there is for his or her understanding of the other actors. The other actors may just be maximising their own preferences or a range of other options. He or she can have no certainty as to the other actor's deliberations and actions. There is no necessary correlation between belief and objective reality. This being the case, we see the usefulness of modelling the PD. The understanding of collective action and collective goals is necessary, I maintain, to understanding the criminal actions, and intent, of criminals acting collectively. The technical work we have looked at is a useful lens for criminologists to employ when addressing the important task of detailing culpable criminal activity.

Bibliography

Amatrudo, A. (2016). Applying Analytical Reasoning to Clarify Intention and Responsibility in Joint Enterprise Cases. *The Politics and Jurisprudence of Group Offending: Onati Socio-Legal Series, 6*(4), 920–936.

Bratman, M. (1984). Two Faces of Intention. *The Philosophical Review, 93*(3), 375–405.

Bratman, M. (1987). *Intentions, Plans and Practical Reason.* Cambridge: Harvard University Press.

Bratman, M. (1992). Shared Cooperative Activity. *The Philosophical Review,* *101*(2), 327–341.

Bratman, M. (1993). Shared Intention. *Ethics, 104*(1), 97–113.

Bratman, M. (1999). *Faces of Intention: Selected Essays on Intention and Agency.* Cambridge: Cambridge University Press.

Brocas, I., Camerer, C., Carrillo, J., & Wang, S. (2014). Imperfect Choice or Imperfect Attention: Understanding Strategic Thinking in Private Information Games. *Review of Economic Studies, 81*(3), 944–970.

Colman, A. (2003). Co-operation, Psychological Game Theory and Limitations of Rationality in Social Interaction. *Behavioral and Brain Sciences, 26*(2), 139–153.

Fleurbaev, M. (2015). Division of Labour in Policy Evaluation: Is There a Role for Normative Analysis. *The Good Society, 24*(1), 73–85.

Gilbert, M. (1999). Obligation and Joint Commitment. *Utilitas, 11*(2), 143–163.

Gilbert, M. (2000). *Sociality and Responsibility: New Essays in Plural Subject Theory.* Lanham: Rowman and Littlefield.

Gilbert, M. (2006). Rationality in Collective Action. *Philosophy of the Social Sciences, 36*(1), 3–17.

Guilfoos, T., & Duus Pape, A. (2016). Predicting Human Cooperation in the Prisoner's Dilemma Using a Case-Based Decision Theory. *Theory and Decision, 80*(1), 1–32.

Hurley, S. (1989). *Natural Reasons.* Oxford: OUP.

Jayasingh, S., & Eze, U. (2015). An Empirical Analysis of Consumer Behavioral Intention Towards Mobile Coupons in Malaysia. *International Journal of Business and Information, 4*(2), 221–242.

List, C., & Petit, P. (2011). *Group Agency: The Possibility, Design and Status of Corporate Agents.* Oxford: OUP.

Roth, A. (2003). Practical Inter-Subjectivity. In F. Schmitt (Ed.), *Socializing Metaphysics; The Nature of Social Reality* (pp. 65–69). New York: Rowman & Littlefield.

Roth, A. (2004). Shared Agency and Contralateral Commitments. *The Philosophical Review, 113*(3), 359–410.

Salsa, S. (2016). *Partial Differential Equations: From Modelling to Theory.* London: Springer.

Searle, J. (1980). The Intentionality of Intention and Action. *Cognitive Science, 4*(1), 47–70.

Sheehy, P. (2006). *The Reality of Social Groups.* Chippenham: Ashgate.

Sugden, R. (2000). Team Preferences. *Economics and Philosophy, 16*(2), 175–204.
Taylor, M. (1987). *The Possibility of Cooperation.* Cambridge: Cambridge University Press.
Tuomela, R. (2005). *We*-intentions Revisited. *Philosophical Studies, 125*(3), 327–369.
Varian, H. (1987). *Intermediate Microeconomics.* London: W.W. Norton Publishers.
Wahl, J. (2016). The Problem of Choice. *Journal of French and Francophone Philosophy, 24*(1), 224–258.
Xiao, E., & Kunreuther, H. (2012). *Punishment and Cooperation in Stochastic Social Dilemmas* (Wharton NBER Working Papers, Number 18458, pp. 1–38).

Section 2

Legal Considerations

3

Mobs, Masses and Treating People as *Groups*

One area that certainly concerns the way individuals are treated as primarily part of a group is that of the demonstration. Individuals on a march, or at a protest, are generally thought of as marchers, or protestors, rather than individuals: at least, they are individuals in the category, or class, of marcher or protestor. No serious attention is paid to the divergent opinions of persons on the same march, or protest, or to considering why, precisely, they came along in the first place. An anti-war march is as likely to consist of pacifists or religiously motivated persons than by members of the radical political left, anarchists or just regular troublemakers. This lack of specificity is a real concern for anyone attending a march, or demonstration, since they are more likely to be seen as part of the group than as an individual, *per se*. This has been dealt with extensively by Kistner in relation to South African criminal law in relation to the demonstrations at the Lonmin Platinum mine in Marikana where individual agency was seemingly waived (Kistner 2015). My worry is that the problem of crowds is simply this; that common purpose may be attributed at any moment in the life of a crowd. Our innate capacity to undertake collective action may be fused, by the public authorities, with a mistaken, and over-simplified, version of human intentionality, in

© The Author(s) 2018
A. Amatrudo, *Criminal Actions and Social Situations*,
https://doi.org/10.1057/978-1-137-45731-8_3

terms of what the crowd, *qua* crowd. The actions of the crowd are deemed unlawful, along with all its constituent members. In this scenario, it will be an uphill battle to distinguish the individual crowd member from the crowd, *qua* crowd, and problematic in terms of practical policing too (Kistner 2015, 33). Moreover, other than to maintain their own good behaviour what can they do, in the eyes of the law, to differentiate themselves from any violent, or unruly, elements in the crowd, and in any case how might they seek to effect that? There is, at the very least, the suspicion that law-abiding and peaceful persons in a crowd may be taken as fellow travellers in any breach of the peace. These are very serious civil liberty concerns at any time but certainly now with people angry at public sector wage freezes, the state of the National Health Service, student fees and a multitude of other causes when people may very well wish to exercise their lawful right to protest. The right to protest is an important democratic element in our democracy. It is, moreover, a crucial aspect of our right to free speech and well won in earlier days. The prioritising of the group, over and against, the individual may well be understandable, even unavoidable. This is not the point in question. The issue is the right of all persons to be thought of as separate and differentiated persons and to be thought of as such. Morrison makes a very important point about the linkage of freedom of speech and rights of assembly (i.e. demonstrations, marches, meetings and so forth) in his seminal article on assembly in the first half of the twentieth century in America: "The period from 1918 to1927 witnessed the widespread use of membership crime, out of which substantive First Amendment rights emerged. While robust speech right would ultimately result, assembly was most often an issue" (Morrison 2015, 754). In the American example, following the First World War, the growing calls for women's suffrage, equality between the races and so forth were attacked primarily through the breaking up of assemblies where people came together to exchange views, support one another and advance strategies for political and social change; similar public order strategies have been employed in different places and at different times: all I am doing here is noting the role of assembly in the political discourse of a nation, and its importance at effecting change. Morrison shows how it is often easier for the state to attack an assembly of persons in a public place than to deal with dissent in published form.

In recent years, the UK government has modified its focus around policing in terms of its attitude towards the whole area of public order, in general, and the control of crowds, especially. This has not so been so much in terms of sports events or cultural and religious events but in terms of public protests, notably in London. This concern, whilst always there, has been heightened since the protests in the Middle East at the time of the Arab Spring and the emergence of the so-called Occupy Movement and it has received a lot of academic as well as media attention. The individual protester is not the concern only the crowd, *qua* crowd. The larger group seems to usurp the life of the everyday man and woman. The economic crisis that hit the world in 2008 seemingly ushered in a new era of protest in its wake and in the UK the student protest of 2010 was a major worry for the public authorities, as was the sight of large numbers of chaotic rioters in the summer of 2011. The state became very concerned about the crowd as a focus for popular dissent and from 2008 there were numerous voices raised in Parliament, in the police and in local government for a new look at the UK's legal framework for addressing *disordered* crowds. It also has to be noted that some of these crowd issues were linked to broader social movements, like the Occupy Movement, which itself is something of a challenge to the hitherto usual way of airing political grievances, Parliament. These movements are largely extra-parliamentary and represent a very real challenge to the usual notion of governmentality and how to change opinion. The social movements of the early twenty-first century appeared to be novel in many ways, though the *tradition* of public demonstration is age-old.

It was felt that the law must have a role in combating what was widely considered an emergent, and threatening, form of political organisation against the state, protesting crowds. Of course, none of this is new and elites have always felt threatened by crowds right back to classical times. The Marxist historian, George Rude, long ago highlighted the terror felt by elites from a *bottom-up* politics driven by ordinary people and which bypasses the existing political structures of change. Though Rude was taken with popular uprisings in the 1730–1848 period, notably in England and France, the issue he focuses upon is a perennial one (Rude 1964). The issue we deal with is that in concentrating upon the agency of the group, the individual agency of individuals is minimised if not neglected altogether; and this, of course, has real consequences in terms of the criminal law and individual human rights. What is often portrayed as a public order issue is, at root, an important element in our civic life; and arguably with the growth of social movements a growing one. In accounting for the life of the crowd we have to: "… (understand) … the complex causation of moments of disorder … to see the actions of the police and the protestors existing in a material, social and cultural context. The crowd responds to police force on the basis of perceptions of legitimacy and victimisation, while the occupational culture of the police 'others' the protestors" (rua Wall 2016, 403).

Kettling Crowds

One may think that it is only radical environmental campaigners, or those involved in political protest, who are negatively affected by police powers in public places in term of the control of crowds but this would be very much mistaken. Modern police crowd control, especially in relation to the tactic of *kettling*, has been the subject of a lot judicial oversight in the higher courts. A good example of this is the case of *Austin and another v Metropolitan Police Commissioner*.[1] In this case the House of Lords looked at the way kettling was employed by the Metropolitan Police, in and around the Oxford Circus area of London, on May Day 2001. The Metropolitan Police saw the tactic in terms of crowd control and argued that the crowds in the area were a threat to public order and had to be *contained*. The crowds were not uniformly hostile and the police themselves accepted that the overwhelming majority of protesters were calm and peaceful. One claimant, Ms Austen, who was one of the protesters was making speeches using a megaphone and she was then deemed to be hostile by the police, who had observed her. The other claimant, claimant S, took no part in the demonstration whatsoever but became, on the afternoon of 1 May 2001, embroiled in the crowd during her regular business, and unavoidably so, given the geographical location of Oxford Circus in terms of it being a thoroughfare and public transport hub; and it was the location of claimant S's site of work. At 2.20pm both Austin and claimant S, along with many others, were prevented by the police from departing from the Oxford Circus area without the express permission of officers on duty. During this period of enforced police detention, both Austin and claimant *S* were extensively filmed and recorded by a specialist Metropolitan Police surveillance unit. The period of detention, in the kettle, lasted almost eight hours during which time no toilet or sanitary facilities were forthcoming and no water or fluids were provided by the public authorities, including the police. Both Austin and claimant *S* subsequently sued the Metropolitan Police for both false imprisonment under the Common Law and under Article 5(1) of the European Convention on Human Rights (ECHR) in relation to their rights to liberty and security. When the case came to trial, the judge sided with the police in holding that the demonstration represented a potentially very dangerous situation and that, to preserve public order and prevent any damage occurring to commercial property, the Metropolitan Police were within their rights to use the kettle to contain any potential trouble. The judge also reasoned, in relation to claimant *S*, that the police were justified in holding the entire group of persons within the kettle since the police maintained that they, collectively, could be thought of as about to commit a breach of the peace in the circumstances that presented on that day. There was an appeal to the Civil Division of the Court of Appeal which upheld all the decisions of the lower court save its holding that all the persons within the kettle could be reasonably understood as being about to commit a breach of the peace. However, in stating that the court determined that in difficult circumstances the police had done what they could necessarily do and so had not themselves breached the Common Law due to the exceptional circumstances pertaining to May Day 2001. Following the unsuccessful ruling from the Court of Appeal, Austin took her claim under Article 5(1) of the European Convention on Human Rights to the House of Lords where it was dismissed on the grounds that Article 5(1) had to be understood in terms of its relationship to Article 2 (the right to life), since the public authorities have a duty to protect the general public from riotous behaviour. Therefore, in determining the rightfulness, or otherwise, of police crowd control measures a balance must be struck between the individual rights of protesters, and those like claimant *S* who inadvertently get caught up in events, and the interests of public order and the safety of the wider community. Moreover, any measures the police undertake need to be proportionate to the real risks of a crowd becoming out of control. In dismissing Austin's claim the House of Lords maintained that, in the circumstances pertaining to the events on May Day 2001, she had not been subject to any arbitrary deprivation of liberty but that she had been contained as part of a wider programme of measures directed at the maintenance of public order and safety.

What is the point we take away from this? For our purposes, the issue is surely that such examples demonstrate the problems implicit in being treated as an individual in what is a dynamic social situation. The issue is where the boundary lies between a duty to respect individual persons and to admit the reality of collective action. Moreover, it underscores the problems that the public authorities have in determining this, especially in fast-moving situations that do not easily lend themselves to close calls of an analytical sort. The duty to treat individuals as separate persons and to, at other times, treat them as a part of a collective and to understand how an individual may be understood as occupying both designations (individual and group member) is a very complex matter, as we saw in the first two chapters of this book. These are not matters that can ever be so simplified as to make them matter-of-fact tools of the public authorities. They may be set out clearly in analytical writing but it is difficult to sustain the notion this can also be the case in matters of policing, notably where disorder is a feature.

If we examine the case of *Austin and another v Metropolitan Police Commissioner* we note the real difficulty a judge often has in determining *individual* culpability in a crowd situation; and how this often leads to over-simplifying matters and to think of the peaceful protestors as acquiescing in the behaviour of the disorderly protestors. Lord Hope sets out one such issue, that of agreeing who is culpable of disorderly conduct, in the context of a kettle: "While about 60% remained calm about 40% were actively hostile, pushing and throwing missiles. Those who were not pushing or throwing missiles were not dissociating themselves from the minority who were" (Austin 2009, 6). Lord Hope is here, I argue, blurring the lines between peaceful protestors and disorderly ones. He seems to hold that the peaceful protestors in the kettle are, in some way, culpable since they fail actively to dissociate themselves from the violent protestors, beyond their own non-violence. One might even hold, on Lord Hope's rationale, that there seems to be common cause between the peaceful protestors and disorderly ones. Much the same was stated in the HMIC Report *Adapting to Protest: nurturing a British model of Policing*: "… crowds are understood as unpredictable, volatile and dangerous, it becomes almost self-evident that they need to be controlled and that this control must be exerted primarily through the use of force. The theoretical position results in police tending to see the general heterogeneous composition of crowds in terms of a simple dichotomy: an irrational majority and a violent minority who can easily assert influence over the crowd" (HMIC 2009, 85). There seems to be a tendency to juxtapose violent protestors with peaceful ones yet to also be rather wary of the innocence of the peaceful ones, who in any case, may succumb to the contagion of the *irrational* life of the crowd. The psychological reasoning at play here seems rather arcane and at odds with what we now know of crowds. Extremely worrying are the words of Lord Neuberger in the case of *Austin and another v Metropolitan Police Commissioner* in which he reasons that when somebody attends a protest, where some form of social unrest may arise, they could be said to have foreseen the possibility of their being confined, in a kettle, and agreed to it "…if imputed consent is an appropriate basis for justifying confinement for Article 5 purposes then it seems to me that the confinement in the present case could be justified on the basis that anyone on the streets, particularly on a demonstration with a well-known risk of serious violence, must be taken to be consenting to the possibility of being confined by the police, if it is a reasonable and proportionate way of preventing serious public disorder and violence" (Austin 2009, 9). This is a rather disturbing line of reasoning coming from such a distinguished judge. Lord Neuberger implicates "anyone on the streets" as being able to foresee, and agree, to their own confinement prior to any public order matters even arising: the possibility is enough. The same goes for those in the kettle at the time of any public disorder. This is *always* to make the persons contained within the kettle the architect of their own confinement, which seems wrong on many levels. This reasoning has the effect, moreover, of discouraging other citizens from taking part in a protest if they could, in any way, foresee some form of disorder breaking out. This notion at work in Lord

Neuberger's opinion is reductive at best and generally wholly inadequate in accounting for the individual actions of persons in a crowd of any sort, the more so in a protest. In discouraging people from taking part in protest it might well also be termed anti-democratic. It entirely misses the sheer complexity of dynamic social situations. The police are never, in the account proffered by Lord Neuberger, in any way conceivably causal in any social unrest. Police tactics during situations of operational crowd control seem devoid of any sociological context and without any analytical framework by which to judge the actions of individuals or of groups being policed (Knight et al. 2013).

Kettling Children

One of the most controversial cases of kettling that involved the UK courts was in 2011 when the courts revisited the whole issue of kettling in relation to a case concerning a sizeable demonstration against student tuition fees in central London, where the police had to use their powers, as it turned out expectantly to involve children. The Metropolitan Police are well-versed in dealing with crowds but, in this instance, they had failed to anticipate the participation of a considerable number of children. The details are supplied in *R (on the application of Castle and others) v Metropolitan Police Commissioner.*[2] The Metropolitan Police set about containing the agitated crowd that presented in the Whitehall area of London a little after 1pm and did endeavour to identify young and vulnerable persons as part of that process; all of which is standard procedure. However, the plaintiffs in the case were a fourteen-year-old girl and two sixteen-year-old boys and they were not let out of the kettle until 7pm and 8.30pm, respectively. The plaintiffs did not sue the Metropolitan Police for false imprisonment, as may have been expected, but instead they invoked Public Law and made an application for a judicial review of the Metropolitan Police's decision to contain them. In doing this, in the first instance, they utilised section 11 of the Children's Act 2004 which imposes a statutory duty upon various public bodies, including the police, and states that they "…must make arrangements for ensuring that their functions are discharged having regard to the need to safeguard and promote the welfare of children." They also drew attention to the very long period of time that the containment was established by the police. The Court's opinion was that section 11 of the Children's Act 2004 did, indeed, require the Metropolitan Police to ensure that their functions are undertaken so as to promote the welfare of young people and that it is also right to hold that the statutory duty was, in turn, determined by both the *function* and *circumstance* of any operation. Moreover, that individual police officers ought not be deterred from exercising their duties simply because of the presence of a child. The Court also held that, as a general principle, any police impediment with the usual norms around the freedom of movement of persons must be specifically justified. Kettling, as a form of containment, can only ever be justified where there are no other alternative measures which could prevent citizens (i.e. third parties not involved in a demonstration) from being drawn into a breach of the peace. Importantly, the Court held that if kettling (containment) is deemed to be the only course of action open to the police then it is lawfully justified if it is deemed operationally necessary; and that it should not be considered excessive even where it is instituted in circumstances where the public authorities had not anticipated the events which brought about institution of the kettling. In the *Castle and others* Case the Court noted that the Metropolitan Police had fully complied with their operational codes of conduct and met their duties to innocent third parties in minimising the impact of the kettling and that they had not unlawfully extended the period of the containment. Kettling was deemed to be no more than a very useful operational tool to be instituted in rare public order instances.

Innocent Victims in Kettles

The *Castle and others* case was significant for what it ruled in relation to third parties in a kettle. It stated that the police have a statutory duty to seek alternatives to kettling as ways to minimise the impact upon third parties. Therefore, the police must always have a plan for alternatives to kettling; at least it has to be formally considered. This exacts a duty on the courts to determine, with a high degree of accuracy, the plans the police have in place around the matter of crowd control as well as the operational institution of those plans; especially where third parties are injured and where civil or criminal claims are made against the police as the statutory public authority. The most notable case in this regard concerns the tragic death of Ian Tomlinson. Tomlinson was an innocent 47-year-old newspaper seller who, during his regular business, was killed as a result of the actions of PC Simon Harwood, a Metropolitan Police officer, during the protests and civil disorder that arose out of the April 2002 London G20 Summit. PC Harwood forcibly pushed Tomlinson and struck him with his baton and he fell to the ground. Tomlinson was not himself a protestor but simply a man trying to negotiate his way home through the series of cordons the Metropolitan Police instituted. After the assault by PC Harwood he collapsed in the street and died just moments later. The death of Ian Tomlinson was later ruled to be an unlawful killing by the Coroner's Inquest held in 2011. Although the police officer, Simon Harwood, was subsequently acquitted of the charge of manslaughter he was nonetheless dismissed from the Metropolitan Police on a charge of gross misconduct in public office (Gearey et al. 2013).

Another incident is worth noting, for anyone thinking of pursuing civil proceedings against the police where personal injury is a concern, is that of the ruling by the House of Lords in the case of *Farrell v Secretary of State for Defence*.[3] In this case a claim for damages was made against the Ministry of Defence by the widow of a man shot to death by the British Army in Northern Ireland. The British Army stated that they had issued two warnings in the form of a call to "Halt" both of which were ignored by Farrell. The dead man, one must point out, had been trying to rob another person who had been attempting to deposit money in a bank's night safe. In the statement Mrs Farrell (the widow) claimed that the soldiers involved in the shooting had been negligent, and used excessive force, in firing their weapons. Mrs Farrell did not claim, however, that there was a question of negligence to put to the senior army officers who had deployed their soldiers correctly in furtherance of anti-terrorist measures, which included the planning of the protection of the bank from robbery and terrorist attack. The case came up at the Northern Ireland High Court before Justice LJ and a serving jury. It held that, in the circumstances pertaining in Northern Ireland, at the time, the soldiers concerned were reasonable to assume that Mr Farrell was indeed a terrorist. Mrs Farrell then took the case to the Court of Appeal in Northern Ireland. The Court of Appeal in Northern Ireland instructed that a new trial be held and that it should also consider the matter of negligence regarding the senior army officers too, thereby making the case much broader in scope. The Ministry of Defence were greatly concerned at this and took an appeal to the House of Lords, which was successful. The decision of the House of Lords was that Gibson LJ was right in his original decision to contain the scope of the case to the soldiers and not widen it to include their superiors in the British Army; and noted that the case should only relate to the persons Mrs Farrell herself had highlighted in her original statement of claim. Moreover, Lord Edmund Davies made the point that, although the courts had the power to amend the terms of a litigant's written statement of plea, it was easy to envisage circumstances where doing this would likely cause an injustice to other parties. Lord Edmund Davies further noted that: "To shrug off a criticism as a 'mere pleading point' is therefore bad law and bad practice. For the primary purpose of pleadings remains, and it can prove of vital importance. That purpose is to define the issues and thereby to inform the parties in advance of the case they have to meet and to enable them to deal with it." It is worth noting here that the Civil Procedure Rules of 1998, and the subsequent amendments to them following Rupert Jackson's Report, similarly underscored the idea that courts must always prioritise how the parties themselves set out the case and the surrounding matters associated with it. In the *Farrell v Secretary of State for Defence* case this is important, for our purposes, since by citing the individual soldiers the case is weighted in terms of considering the actions of two persons. This would not have been the case if the actions of senior British Army officers, the corporate body, had been included. Therefore, we can say that *Farrell v Secretary of State for Defence* is a case that focused upon the culpability of individuals not groups of individuals. It is also easier to understand how the deliberations and actions of the soldiers in question are a much simpler matter to decide than that of a broader, more amorphous, group; in this case, senior British Army officers not present at the event in question.

The So-called *Cordon Sanitaire* in Parliament Square

Along with the phenomenon of kettling another issue has arisen in British public life: the powers of the police to tightly control Parliament Square, which at once is both a major tourist spot and a road juncture. It is, moreover, directly outside the Houses of Parliament. This has become an even more pressing matter following the terrorist attack on Westminster Bridge and subsequent stabbing to death of a police officer on guard duty at the entrance to Parliament in 2017. The Metropolitan Police have broad powers over the conduct of demonstrations and, to that end, generally deny unauthorised demonstrations in Parliament Square, and the surrounding area, even when such demonstrations may be peaceful. This also includes demonstrations by individuals, who act alone, and are not linked to any larger group. The Metropolitan Police were granted these very wide powers by the Serious Organised Crime and Police Act 2005, specifically sections 132–138. These powers came about due to the actions of one man, Brian Haw. His extended, arguably infamous, lone campaign of protest, started in June 2001, against the British government's military actions in Iraq consisted of him living on the pavement in Parliament Square across from the Houses of Parliament. Initially, in 2002, the local council, Westminster City Council, took action against Haw in the High Court to evict him from Parliament Square.[4] This action against Haw failed and the judge in the case, Gray J, maintained that Haw, far from acting unlawfully was merely expressing his freedom of expression under Article 10 ECHR and as set out in *Nagey v Weston* 1965.[5] Indeed, that Haw's action was no worse than other lawful activity, such as selling food from a stationary vehicle, or collecting money for charity in the street, or distributing leaflets, or a whole host of other activities. As a direct result of Brian Haw's ongoing demonstration over the British government's military involvement in Iraq, section 138(2) of the 2005 Act, which allows for the prohibition of demonstrations by the Secretary of State within a *cordon sanitaire* (i.e. an area designated of up to 1 kilometre from, and including, Parliament Square) was pursued by the authorities. However, this broad *cordon sanitaire* proved rather more difficult to enact than had been originally thought and the then Home Secretary, Charles Clarke, had to determine the *cordon sanitaire* to mean all of Parliament Square, including the pavements, but not the buildings that adjoined the pavements. Since the area of the *cordon sanitaire* was so large it would have also included the pavements up as far as Trafalgar Square had these not been specifically referred to in, and excluded from, the statutory instrument that enacted the *cordon sanitaire* because of the intervention of Baroness Scotland of Asthal.[6] The 2005 Act, specifically section 132(1), saw the creation of a completely new method of breaching the *cordon sanitaire* by way of organising, or in any way being party to, a demonstration anywhere in the designated area without the express authorisation of the public authorities. Moreover, it also created a duty on the Metropolitan Police Commissioner to authorise such demonstrations as were allowed under section 134(2) of the 2005 Act. Any notices, under the 2005 Act, must be issued by the police six days before the commencement of any demonstration, where practicable, and never less than 24 hours prior to the start of any demonstration. In addition to this, the Metropolitan Police Commissioner was placed under a duty not only to authorise demonstrations but to specify special conditions where this is done to prevent disorder from breaking out within the *cordon sanitaire*. Of course, these risks did not really relate to Brian Haw. Nonetheless, Caroline Flint, the then Parliamentary Under-Secretary of State for the Home Department, related to Parliament that police officers were instructed to "check behind paraphernalia for devices left, not by people who are protesting, but by people who might use the protest for their own motives to cause a security problem."[7]

Brian Haw the *Pre-existing* Demonstrator in the Parliament Square *Cordon Sanitaire*

The 2005 Act's sections regarding the notice needed for the granting of authorisations for demonstrations were enacted in July 2005 by an earlier commencement order made in June of the same year.[8] The final sections of the Act (i.e. sections 132–137) were enacted in August 2005. The wording of the commencement order stated "demonstrations starting" and in section 132(1) and section 133(2) this clearly refers to demonstrations "starting or continuing" on or after 1 August 2005. Of course, Brian Haw's demonstration had begun much earlier, in 2001. Blake has set out this saga in some considerable detail (Blake 2008). Haw successfully argued that his demonstration had been in uninterrupted operation for four years so his case fell outside of the act (Blake 2008). In the case of *Westminster City Council v Haw* the judge read from Brian Haw's original statement in which he stated that he protests on a full 24-hour basis. The judge in the case noted how Haw "sleeps and eats" on the pavement itself. The legal case that Haw mounted was all about his demonstration preceding the Act and his *right* therefore to continue with it after July 2005. A literal understanding of the law would seem to side with Haw but a view might be discerned in terms of a broader legislative purpose to stripping Haw of his existing rights of protest and beyond that his *home*, since he lived 24 hours a day on the Parliament Square pavement, and to deprive him, furthermore, of any compensation following eviction. Instead of awaiting prosecution Haw, and his legal team, made a petition to the Divisional Court of the High Court in July 2005 for a ruling against both the Home Secretary and the Metropolitan Police Commissioner, and granting that the contents of the 2005 Act did not, and could not, apply to him given his protect began many years earlier. Haw's application was successful, though with a dissention from Simon J.[9] It is important to note here that the way the Home Secretary had interpreted the Act would have had the effect of turning Haw's long-standing, and lawful, demonstration, which needed no authorisation, into a criminal action. How could Haw be guilty of engaging in an activity without permission where there was no requirement to gain any permission? A similar reasoning held in the decision of the House of Lords in the case of *Waddington v Mia*. In that case, the defendant was unable to be found guilty of doing something which required no permission at the time of his doing it; in that case, entering the UK without leave. There was an appeal to the Civil Division of the Court of Appeal. The Court of Appeal was swayed by the more purposive treatment of the 2005 Act, preferred by the government, in determining the legislation that related to the *cordon sanitaire* surrounding Parliament Square. In its judgment, the Court of Appeal maintained that the 2005 Act should be understood as expressing the intention of the government that it should apply to demonstrations that started before the commencement of its powers "as surely as [to] those starting after."[10] Brian Haw was denied his appeal to the House of Lords against this ruling.[11] Blake has argued how Haw was, in June 2005, the sole individual to have established rights to eat and sleep and to reside on the pavement in Parliament Square (Blake 2008, 183). Moreover, that he had secured those rights under Article 10 ECHR during his High Court battle with Westminster City Council.[12] Haw was unique in being placed outside of those persons in a category, or class, by sections 132–138 of the Serious Organised Crime and Police Act 2005 since the category, or class, referred to future persons to be covered in terms of their applying to the police for the correct authorisation prior to their demonstration beginning. The important technical point to note here is this: Parliament certainly could deprive Haw of his existing rights. It is sovereign and can make such laws as it sees fit, under Law. The problem for Parliament was simply that if it sought to take away Haw's rights, in other words, if that was its express wish, for whatever reason, then it would need to bring the entire procedure forward in what is termed a hybrid bill. The use of a hybrid bill would then allow Haw to make his case to Parliament through the committee system that is established in both the Commons and the Lords, since he was being considered "… in a manner different from the private or local interests of other persons or bodies in the same category, so as to, attract the provisions of the standing orders applicable to private business" (Mackay 2004, 566). This is without touching upon Article 8 ECHR (respect for private and family life) and Article 1 of the First Protocol to the ECHR (peaceful enjoyment of *possessions*). It is clear that the Common Law and Article 7 ECHR specifically outlaw retroactive *criminal* legislation. The Common Law, moreover, works with a presumption of title, in other words that an individual's property may not be usurped or damaged by the Crown, including during war time, without compensation, unless it is expressly excluded by an Act of Parliament.[13] However, it may seem odd that a person can claim, nonetheless, that their home is on the pavement, as was the opinion of Gray J in *Westminster City Council v Haw*, and similarly in respect of the facts in *R (on the application of Haw) v Home Secretary*. The more so since Article 10 ECHR prevented Haw from being considered as a person who was obstructing "without lawful authority or excuse", contrary to section 137 of the Highways Act 1980, or even his being considered as a rough sleeper contrary to section 4 of the Vagrancy Act 1824. It was held that Haw's *political* placards, which he used to maintain his protest even when briefly away from the pavement, were not to be considered advertisements and so did not breach the Control of Advertisement Regulations or section 224 of the Town and Country Planning Act 1990. The authorities in Parliament and in Westminster City Council, after the case of *Westminster City Council v Haw* and the decision of the Court of Appeal in *R (on the application of Haw) v Home Secretary*, decided that there was only one way of getting rid of Haw from Parliament Square and that was to offer to pay him proper compensation. The drafters of the 2005 Act had neither foreseen the example of an existing protest nor thought of protests other than in *group* terms. Brian Haw was the exception to both these, in what proved for the public purse, very costly oversights.

In legislation subsequent to the Brian Haw in Parliament Square case controls over demonstration were further added to in Part 5 of the Police and Social Responsibility Act 2011. This enabled the police and other *authorised officers*, usually local authority staff, the right to outlaw both temporary structures and the use of amplification in Parliament Square. In the case of *R (on the application of Gallestequi) v Westminster City Council* the High Court maintained that despite a protestor having permission to protest from the public authorities, in this case the Metropolitan Police Commissioner under section 134 of the Serious Organised Crime and Police Act 2005, this could nonetheless be compensated for by completely different objectives related to the 2011 Act as could a protestor's rights under the ECHR, specifically Articles 6, 10 and 11.[14] The upshot of the 2011 Act is to maintain that the restrictions in that Act are proportionate and should be weighed against other criteria. What this means, in effect, is that local authorities can exercise their powers under the 2011 Act because they are the correct, and most appropriate, authority to exercise those powers in their area. Indeed, one may argue, it is specifically in such sorts of cases that we see the role of local authorities most clearly. Local authorities have very widespread powers under section 222 of the

Local Government Act 1972 to seek injunctions to end any type of public nuisance or breach of the Common Law in their designated area. We note how during the Occupy Movement's anti-capitalism protests in 2012 that when protestors *occupied* the pavements that were legally an aspect of the public highway around St. Paul's Cathedral the local authority, in that case the City of London Corporation, pursued an action for possession of those pavements and duly sought injunctions to remove the tents that had been erected on nearby land. In the court action that followed, the Civil Division of the Court of Appeal upheld the rights of the City of London Corporation and considered that it was reasonable, when considering the rights of protest and lawful assembly, that due weight be given to matters of time and space, especially the duration of the protest in question and its physical extent. The location, and extent, that protestors choose has to be weighed against the *bona fide* legal rights of members of the public to go about their business and the rights of landowners. In the case of the Occupy Movement protests, the City of London Corporation was successful in their action because it could be readily demonstrated to the court that the Occupy Movement protest presented a clear case of significant interference with the lawful rights of citizens to go about their business and it could be shown that it presented a contravention of the Highways Act 1980. As the protestors were sleeping out and had no organised sanitation or running water, given its duration, it also breached a great deal of public health legislation, both UK and EU.[15]

The Surveillance of Campaigners and the Powers of the Police

The state wherever it is situated will need, from time to time, to undertake surveillance upon certain people and certain groups. In recent years there appears to have been a broadening of this necessary function of state security when applied to terrorist, and similarly serious, cases, and to take in more contentious persons and groups; those who normally would not be thought of as threat to society, such as environmental campaigners and those involved in local political protests around such issues as the closing of a hospital or the diminution of services to the elderly or to support childcare. The argument has often been of the slippery slope sort wherein an escalation is posited, a false logic invoked. Environmental activists have at times sought to buy shares, sometimes just a single share, in a public listed company displaying behavior that they disapprove of to gain access to shareholder meetings so they can readily gain access to meetings and can disrupt proceedings. This has happened at several high-profile annual general meetings (AGMs). Although such share-holding protestors do cause disruption and can be thrown out by security staff this tactic raises a great many questions about the status of the shareholding protestors. Are they shareholders first or are they better understood as protestors? Do the police have the right to question, inconvenience and detain protestors who are also shareholders? Moreover, presumably their shareholder status is prior to any disruption undertaken. How can the police intervene against minority shareholders in their dispute against majority shareholders, in a private meeting? One notes the difficulties this situation throws up and its possible misuse by majority shareholders against legitimate dissenters, leaving aside any matters of outside political protest. Moreover, what difference does it make if a given shareholder is motivated by political as opposed to commercial, ethical or financial reasons; and how would one set about disentangling those reasons, one from the other, if it were a consideration? The case of *R (on the application of Wood) v Metropolitan Police Commissioner* is instructive here and it is noteworthy that Wood was a long-standing campaigner against the international arms trade.[16] Wood, though active in various campaigns against the arms trade, had no criminal convictions and had never previously been arrested by the police. Wood was at an AGM as a shareholder, having previously bought one share in the company, when he was photographed by the police who were involved in surveillance and evidence-gathering activity against protestors. When the meeting was concluded Wood, along with several of his fellow campaigners, made his way to the underground station and there the whole group were formally asked to identify themselves to the police. They all refused to do this. The police officers involved in the operation retained the photographs and later Wood was identified. Following this occurrence, he sought judicial review, under Article 8 ECHR, respect for private and family life, in order that the police officers concerned had their conduct examined in terms of their taking photographs in the first place and then retaining them. Wood's application for a judicial review was subsequently rejected by the High Court and he appealed to the Civil Division of the Court of Appeal. The Court of Appeal noted that rights under Article 8 ECHR related to the notion of a *reasonable expectation of privacy*: in other words, was Wood right to expect his right to privacy in the setting in question? In the *Wood* case, there seemed to be no *reasonable* explanation as to why the police took, and retained, photographs of an ordinary man, with no prior criminal history, going about his normal business in the city he lives. The police, at the time, gave no explanation of their conduct but later argued that photographing Wood was part of a wider pre-identification procedure of persons they believed might go on to disrupt a major upcoming arms expo. In the *Wood* case, the Court of Appeal reasoned that Wood clearly had had his Article 8 rights infringed. As to the question of whether, or not, this infringement was warranted for other reasons by the police, the court reasoned that taking photographs of persons, for the sole purpose of preventing public disorder, or to protect and preserve the rights of other citizens, was a legitimate police activity under Article 8(2) ECHR. The Court of Appeal had then to decide whether, in the *Wood* case, an individual's rights, under Article 8 ECHR, was proportionate to the preventive determination on risk, cited in Article 8(2) ECHR. In a majority decision, it ruled that there is clearly a distinction to be drawn between serious crime, or the prevention of terrorist activity, and the sort of everyday minor disruption that is part and parcel of living in a democratic state. It concluded that the taking and retaining of photographs, even if only for a few days, had in this case only been done because the police had an idea, a hunch, that Wood may later go on to disrupt a major upcoming arms expo, several months hence. This rationale was rejected by the Court of Appeal. The police, after all, had not undertaken this evidence gathering and photographic record of persons for any reason associated with the shareholder AGM. It all seemed rather speculative on the police's part and so the Court of Appeal held that the police activity in question was unlawful, being both disproportionate and a straightforward case of infringing Wood's rights to privacy under Article 8 ECHR.

Thinking About Crowds

This is not as straightforward as it appears. Is there a distinction to be had between a group of people and a crowd? At what point does a crowd become purposive or act mob-like? These are questions that the Marxist historian Eric Hobsbawm dealt with in his seminal *Primitive Rebels* (Hobsbawm 1964; rua Wall 2016). Hobsbawm, of course, was looking at the matter of public disorder to discern purposive *political* action not criminality, as such. In Marxist terms, Hobsbawm's task was to see whether, and in what economic circumstances, a crowd represents a *class-in-itself* or a *class-for-itself* (Andrew 1983). In the nineteenth century, especially, crowds were worrisome to the ruling classes of Europe. They seemed to represent a powerful and aggressive force likely to overthrow civic order. Crowds were understood as potentially savage things and a great deal of our public order legislation emanates from the nineteenth century and the panic around crowds, and their supposed potential for unrest, at the time. Today, we have a much more nuanced set of ideas about crowds be they at music festivals or commercially driven, such as in crowd sourcing. Crowds are no longer to be uniformly feared (Surowiecki 2004; rua Wall 2016). There is nothing new in our change of thinking about crowds; as law and society changes it throws up new ways to negotiate dissent and work through non-parliamentary views about our evolving democratic landscape. As we saw, in relation to joint enterprise crime, the law, nonetheless, seems to have problems dealing with complex matters involving several parties. Moreover, it tends to overlook the underlying networks of history and culture that permeate any social situation, and certainly this holds in the case of a protest demonstration. This neglect also seems to overlook the police as a causal agent who are usually only thought of, in turn, as coming in after the fact of the crime, breach or some such. There is no serious consideration given to the way the police are understood, or that the role of the police is in any way contentious: ideas about police legitimacy or protestor victimisation are given scant regard. In a dynamic sociological space, that of the protest, the *othering* of protestors by the police forms no formal part of any judicial process; instead the police are generally portrayed as neutral agents with no skin in the game, as it were. Moreover, when the police do move in and arrest somebody during a protest there is a neglect of matters, such as race and religion, which may play into an underlying narrative of prejudice and unwarranted victimisation. The crowd is, of its nature, a heterogeneous creature and the *good* and the *bad* are all mixed together. It also changes its composition over time. The crowd is inherently unstable, in a formal sense, and liable to alter in its mood from moment to moment. The behaviour of the crowd at $t1$ is no clue whatsoever to its behaviour at $t2$. Though this undoubtedly is the case, by overlooking the ways in which the actions of one group, the police, may alter the behaviour of another group, the crowd, is never given a proper weighting in the understanding of the actions of crowds (Drury and Reicher 2000). What, in the example of the kettle, is represented as a mechanism for order is really a mechanism through which the police can ignore the heterogeneous nature of the crowd and treat everyone the same, though not are all equally deserving. However, the power of the kettle, and police tactics generally, are not typically seen as casual. The fact that the kettle itself may turn the *good* into *bad*, or at least affect the behaviour of the protestors in question, is at best underplayed. The defence of the kettle by the police is always in terms of its facilitating the capture of the *bad* and the freeing of the *good*, as if this was an easy, even clinical, operation. A good example of the police's reasoning is given in the case of *Castle v Metropolitan Police Commissioner* which sets out, in detail, how the kettle is designed to *boil* the crowd. The crowd being contained will become agitated and unable to leave, and surrounded by police in body full armour, is at once an observable space for the police to decided who is, and who is not, a violent protestor.[17] The problem here is obvious; the police caused a great deal of frustration by employing the kettle as a tactic in the first place. Moreover, the violence within the kettle is not necessarily coterminous with any unrest prior to the institution of the kettle. The police may well have caused the behaviour they are supposedly there to deal with. What the kettle does do very effectively is to restrict the area the police are in control of in terms of physical space. In media terms too, it has the helpful by-product of focusing attention on to the dense and *boiling* crowd. The police are seen to be containing the unruly mob. The mob seemingly irrational and out of control is a given. Its prior form, which may have been peaceful, is rarely considered.

The kettle certainly plays well on television for the police, which is an increasingly important consideration in recent times.

A Way Forward?

It seems clear that there are many issues relating to the policing of demonstrations, and that our current legal settlement is not always up to the task it was set. It is certainly the case that the whole area of crowd dynamics and the fluidity of groups is pretty much absent in the public law account. Therefore, we have the lawful democratic rights of protestors on the one hand and on the other the demand for public order and for the rights of ordinary citizens to go about their everyday lives. These rights are supported in public law and deeply rooted in jurisprudence and an elaborated human rights discourse, whilst other claims are indebted to political action and sociological theory. The problem is simply that a lot of law is too abstract and detached to capture the dynamics of a demonstration; at the very least it comes with its own heavy baggage and established terminology. It is not generally set up to notice the complexities of a changing political landscape nor to see the importance of matters at hand. As Lobban noted, in the case of nineteenth-century demonstrations, we need to be aware of the complex interplay of political action and the legal process (Lobban 1990, 306–308; rua Wall 2016, 412). The courts need to be aware that the novelty of today is tomorrow's norm. Moreover, as a society changes so does its means of political expression and the things it holds dearest. We must be wary of demonising the crowd and of creating criminals out of genuine protestors (Stott and Drury 2000). The danger of the kettle is simply that it is a mechanism for producing anxiety, often with associated violence: yet when the violence that the kettle produces is used either by way of instituting a prosecution, or simply for data storage, then something seems wrong. The notion of *good* and *bad* protestors is hardly the point if the violence in question is within the kettle. The kettle may well be a legitimate police tactic but we must be alive to the fact that it can criminalise the crowd and generate its own crimes through its anxiety-driven mechanism of containment. If a person takes part in violent disorder during a protest that is one matter, but it is another altogether if they engage in violent disorder because of the kettle itself. This is surely a form of entrapment. What I suggest is not some vast overhaul of public law nor some version of anarchy but simply more self-awareness of the sort Lobban drew our attention to. The 2010 student protests, against fees, for example, is now part of the Labour Party manifesto and if we have a new government, then will be part of government policy. An awareness of the fluidity of groups and of social norms would go a long way to addressing many of the issues that public order policing has thrown up in recent years. There must be more awareness too of the dangers of the kettling tactics used by the police, notably the Metropolitan Police, and the likelihood of creating a form of violence that was never part of the protest. Finally, beyond all of this, a sense of democracy on the part of the public authorities would be welcomed; by which I mean, protestors and police need to be aware that they both occupy, more or less, the same political space. In terms of a theoretical framework for working on such matters surely rua Wall is right to point us towards a hybrid approach; one that combines the legal with insights from sociology and psychology in his so-called *law of crowds* model (rua Wall 2016, 410–414). He argues:

> … alongside this first sense of being subject to law, we can also identify the 'law of crowds' as a way of thinking about the crowd as the creative agent that produces new law (the law that crowds create or perhaps take possession of). This is the relation between the crowd (as *turba, multitudo* and *vulgus*) and the people; it is a way of thinking about constituent power as both revolt and augmentation. The 'law of crowds' is thus a way of thinking about recent events, such as Occupy, the Arab Spring, the *Indignados* and all of the other crowd phenomena around the world. It frames the law as the site of a series of creative and destructive processes. It is careful with the legal nuance, while refusing to be confronted by the claims to pure normativity without exception …. (it) is nothing less than a different way of thinking about the question of democracy itself. (rua Wall 2016, 414)

I think rua Wall is right here and that the law alone seems inadequate to the task of accounting for the multitude of dynamic political and social action that constitutes any crowd.

Notes

1. *Austin and another v Metropolitan Police Commissioner* [2009] UKHL 5; [2009] 2 WLR 3.
2. *R (on the application of Castle and others) v Metropolitan Police Commissioner* [2011] EWHC 2317 (Admin); [2012] 1 All ER 953.
3. *Farrell v Secretary of State for Defence* [1980] 1 WLR 172; [1980] 1 All ER 166.
4. *Westminster City Council v Haw* [2002] EWHC 2073 (QB).
5. *Nagey v Weston* [1965] 1 WLR 280; [1965] 1 All ER 78.
6. *Hansard,* (HL) vol. 671, col. 770 (Baroness Scotland of Asthal).
7. *Hansard* (HC) 7 February 2005, col. 1291.
8. Serious Organised Crime and Police Act 2005 (Commencement No. 1, Transitional and Transitory Provisions) Order 2005, SI 2005/1521 (C66).
9. *R (on the application of Haw) v Home Secretary* [2005] EWHC 2061 (Admin); [2006] QB 359.
10. *R (on the application of Haw) v Home Secretary* [2006] EWCA Civ 532; [2006] QB 780 [24].
11. [2007] 1 All ER xix.
12. *Westminster City Council v Haw* [2002] EWHC 2073 (QB).
13. *Burmah Oil Co v Lord Advocate* [1965] AC 75.
14. [2012] EWHC 1123 (Admin); [2012] 4 All ER 401.
15. *City of London Corporation v Samede and others* [2012] EWCA Civ 160; [2012] 2 All ER 1039.
16. [2009] EWCA Civ 414; [2009] 4 All ER 951.
17. *Castle v Metropolitan Police Commissioner* [2011] EWCA 2317.

Bibliography

Andrew, E. (1983, September). Class in Itself and Class Against Capital: Karl Marx and His Classifers. *Canadian Journal of Political Science/Revue canadienne de science politique, 16*(3), 577–584.
Blake, L. (2008). Hybrid Bills and Human Rights: The Parliament Square Litigation 2002–2007. *Kings Law Journal, 19,* 183–192.
Drury, J., & Reicher, S. (2000). Collective Action and Psychological Change: The Emergence of New Social Identities. *British Journal of Social Psychology, 39*(4), 579–604.

Gearey, A., Morrison, W., & Jago, R. (2013). *The Politics of the Common Law: Perspectives, Rights, Processes, Institutions.* London: Routledge.

HMIC. (2009). *Adapting to Protest: Nurturing a British Model of Policing.* London: HMIC.

Hobsbawm, E. (1964). *Primitive Rebels.* Manchester: Manchester University Press.

Kistner, U. (2015). Common Purpose: The Crowd and the Public. *Law Critique, 26,* 27–43.

Knight, S., Goold, M., & Elliott, E. (2013). New Threat to the Right to Protest: Stephen Knight on the New Arrest Tactic to Include Legal Observers and Michael Goold and Emily Elliott on an Important Victory in the High Court Against the Met Police and Its Kettling Actions. *Socialist Lawyer, 65*(October), 14–17.

Lobban, M. (1990). From Seditious Libel to Unlawful Assembly; Peterloo and the Changing Face of Political Crime c.1770–1820. *Oxford Journal of Legal Studies, 10*(3), 307–352.

Mackay, W. (2004). *Erskine May's Treatise on the Law, Privileges and Usage of Parliament* (23rd ed.). London: Butterworths.

Morrison, S. (2015). Membership Crime v. The Right to Assemble. *John Marshall Law Review, 48*(3), 729–755.

Rude, G. (1964). *The Crowd in History.* New York: Wiley & Sons.

Stott, C., & Drury, J. (2000). Crowds, Context and Identity: Dynamic Categorization Processes in the Poll Tax Riot. *Human Relations, 53*(2), 247–273.

Surowiecki, J. (2004). *The Wisdom of Crowds.* London: Abacus Books.

rua Wall, I. (2016). The Law of Crowds. *Legal Studies, 36*(3), 395–414.

4

Organisations and Their *Enterprise* in UK Criminal Law and in International Law

The Determination of Responsibility *Vis-a-vis* the Individual and the Corporate Body

The determination of responsibility, *vis-à-vis* the individual and the corporate body is, of its nature, a tricky matter simply because groups are made up of collections of individual members, however fleetingly. How then might a corporate body be said to have intention or any sort of agency, *qua* corporate body? There are questions of responsibility to be settled and the determination must fall somewhere, so we need a theoretical approach that is both plausible and practicable in the large number of cases where this determination of responsibility, *vis-à-vis* the individual and the corporate body, is in question. In the technical section of this book, Chaps. 1 and 2, we looked primarily at analytical tools for determining collective action as it relates to some, fairly, standard cases of joint agency. However, whilst an analytical approach is one I hold to it is, perhaps, not as practically useful as an approach which looks more towards sociological insights, meaning empirically observable ones rather than philosophical ones. Here, I have in mind thinking about

© The Author(s) 2018
A. Amatrudo, *Criminal Actions and Social Situations*,
https://doi.org/10.1057/978-1-137-45731-8_4

these questions in the context of, if you like, a more *organisational* framework. By focusing upon the nature of a social organisation, network even, it will be possible to look at interactions between persons and thereby *attribute* responsibility in terms of the organisational framework, or structure. The sort of sociological questions I have in mind here are along the lines of (1) what do we know about the functioning, or operation, of the organisation in question and (2) what is the role of individuals within the organisation? This sort of model was, of course, used in the prosecution of Nazi war criminals after the Second World War utilising the Nuremberg Protocols. It has also been extensively used in the prosecution of organised crime and prosecution of white-collar crime, notably in the world of banking. It does, though, still prioritise the culpability of *individuals*, observed in terms of their role in the organisation, rather than organisations, *per se*: though the *criminal organisation* nonetheless remains a possibility it is generally understood as being constituted by freely-acting agents. Of course, we might reason that an organisation, *qua* organisation, acting purposively and for legal purposes can be said to possess criminal responsibility and therefore liability. What is altogether unavoidable here at the outset is the realisation that such matters are as much determined by philosophical and sociological reflection than they are simply in terms of the criminal law. The allocation of responsibility in such matters, where individual agency operates within an organisational framework, will always be complex. One thinks here of the response of the many senior Nazis who did not so much deny their guilt as deny the appropriateness of the charges put before them. In the context of their operating within a complex operational, military command, structure they argued that they were only, themselves, responsible for their small role in the overall process of annihilation (Earl 2013a). When faced with charges of mass murder they tended to reply: "Im sinne der Anklage nicht Schuldig" (In the sense of the accusation, not guilty). Eichmann famously claiming only to have organised the trains to Auschwitz and not the extermination of people upon disembarkation and therefore the charges put to him were mistaken in law. Did these Nazis believe in their *limited* liability defence? Whilst rejecting, based on a multitude of documentary and testimonial evidence, the defence Eichmann, and others, mounted of their role in the Holocaust we must nonetheless be alive to the issue of attributing too much responsibility to persons within an organisational structure. The over-attribution of responsibility to an individual is a major concern for justice; but one that a more sociological approach can readily accommodate with reference to the operation of the organisation in question (Earl 2013b).

What is useful to our theorising about these matters is the realisation that in these matters human interaction between individuals and human interaction between individuals and the organisation (its rules, it processes) may be observed. The way an individual operates within an organisation and the way an individual interprets the many rules and regulations, and the ways in which individuals come to see their role, is very telling, and open to objective observation and determination. It goes without saying that although organisations are not human beings they are apt to behave in ways akin to persons and, by way of example, a great deal of modern economics is based on this understanding. The modelling of economic systems certainly has overtones of anthropomorphism too (Tosun et al. 2016, 10). Much the same may be said of the way the relationship between states is modelled in terms of interests and cultural dominance (Gowa and Mansfield 2004). In contemporary political theory, the recent development of game theory also has this attribute (List and Petit 2011). It is not uncommon for us to understand corporate bodies, or other sorts of organisations, as having this form of *identity*, or *nature*, or at least to imagine that, though not themselves flesh and blood, they have a nature that is analogous to that of flesh and blood persons. The issue we will deal with is this: is the organisation analogous *enough* to flesh and blood persons to count as having a form of agency, and therefore responsibility, distinct *enough* from the actors *within* it, or who comprise it, sufficient for it to be distinctly criminally culpable, *qua* organisation? The agency, and distinct form of criminal liability, of financial organisations has been disputed for centuries and shows no sign of resolving itself, as the absence of prosecutions following the 2008 global financial debacle illustrates (Pontell et al. 2014). The matter is often couched in terms of *governance*, by which I understand as meaning, in large part, the parameters placed on the agency of an organisation, i.e. a *non*-human actor, by a range of human actors (Blickle et al. 2006). For our purposes, this is a tight *working* definition of governance.

Determining Appropriate Responsibility

Any model we might devise that addresses the issue of responsibility and the role of both individuals and organisations has necessarily to be built upon a notion of agency that can determine the ways in which both individuals and organisations act and can similarly attribute responsibility, accurately, on that basis. This is no simple task, especially when organisations are heterogeneous, both between themselves and over time. Individuals are altogether more straightforward to model. However, the attribution of responsibility to organisations is an important task and one resting upon addressing both why we should hold an abstract entity, such as an organisation, culpable, rather than a flesh and blood person, and how we are to think of this abstract entity having a form of agency separate from flesh and blood persons (Erskine 2003). Traditionally, this has been attempted in two main ways. Firstly, by thinking of the organisation as having its own form of moral agency and this has often been the way scholars have sought to understand the firm acting in the marketplace or in terms of the moral and ethical responsibility of organisations, as in the case of war crimes, for example the *SS-Einsatzgruppen Prozess* following the Second World War (Earl 2013b). Secondly, jurists have often sought to address legal responsibility in terms of norms that are derived from legal order and judged against that measure. This I hold to be a form of legal positivism and Kelsen is often cited as one of the proponents of such an approach. The former approach is to be preferred with its richer sociological appreciation but it is worth noting Kelsen's words in relation to the latter approach: "(The) imputation to a juristic person is a juristic construction, not the description of a natural reality. It is therefore not necessary to make the hopeless attempt to demonstrate that the juristic person is a real being, not a legal fiction, in order to prove that delicts and especially crimes can be imputed to a juristic person" (Kelsen 1999, 104). In Kelsen's view, the matter of criminal responsibility is to be understood purely by way of reference to law with a rather reductive arbitrary dichotomy between international law, for issues between states, and that of individual states, that deal with issues within their jurisdiction. Kelsen leaves no room for the sociological observable instance which might well show us the ways in which individuals interrelate whether simply between actors or in terms of an organisation. This, more sociological, approach starts from empirically observed reality, not the legal positivism of Kelsen and others in that tradition. Moreover, such a sociological approach will also allow us to determine the agency of a given organisation and, therefore, its responsibility. Here we will rely, from now on, upon the work of Dan-Cohen, notably as set out in his classic essay "Between Selves and Collectivities: Towards a Jurisprudence of Identity" (Dan-Cohen 1994). Dan-Cohen essentially views the human subject as the exemplar of the responsible legal personality and this serves as the model for the ways in which we go on to think about organisations of various kinds. This usefully opens up the door for us to begin to reason about the responsibility of organisations and yet avoid the obvious pitfall of anthropomorphism in relation to organisations.

Before all else, for us to begin to speculate about a distinct organisational actor we need to have in place a reasonably stable underlying structure, if only to achieve the objective of conceiving of such an actor persisting in time and having a full sense of internal consistency to its person. Only when these things are in place may we determine how this organisational actor can link together its constituent human parts and purposively direct them, being both a framework for this flesh and blood interaction and its *conditio sine qua non*. This organisational actor, moreover, must be able to furnish its own sense of internal decision making as the basis for the actions that it undertakes. This view has a long-standing tradition in philosophy but it is also the way business has come to understand the action of companies (Gupta et al. 2017). When these elements are in place—(1) a stable underlying structure and (2) some sense of internal decision making—then we can apply this view to thinking about legal responsibility of various sorts, from companies and official bodies and to states, on the one hand, and to looser and deviant organisations, such as terrorist groups, on the other. The main element, assuming stability, is the sense of internal decision making, since that would appear to determine, above all else, what we might term the *character* of the organisation. This sense of the character in decision-making processes of the organisation is, of course, most at play when we come to determine the culpability, or otherwise, of a given organisation. An organisation is typically established to advance a goal, or set of goals. It has what is technically termed a defined purpose which may be detected in its actions. The agency of the organisation is tied to its purpose, and its purpose may be observed. In such a way, we may see how one organisation exhibits bona fide observable traits whilst another may exhibit illegitimate ones. This form of agency, as expressed in terms of its purposiveness, may also clarify the actions of the organisation, *qua* organisation, rather than the actions of its constituent members which may, though, express it. In this way, we may think of responsibility as primarily relating to the organisation and not the flesh and blood persons, acting either alone or in partnership, that constitute the organisation. In this way, the moral and legal responsibility may be understood in terms of organisations. However, we note that here, as we noted earlier, a stable underlying structure will be at work in determining the actions of flesh and blood persons, though the structure itself does not necessarily possess any physical attributes of note.

We have established that it is possible to think of organisations as having all the necessary features for the attribution of responsibility and yet there does seem to be a certain circularity that we have, thus far, not admitted to. Organisations may shape the actions of persons but the reverse is also true and this would, perhaps, make us wary of coming down entirely on one side or the other. Moreover, we have so far said nothing of choice making, moral or otherwise. Choice making is important in determining responsibility; indeed, it is the choice to follow one course of action rather than another that is in question when accounting for it. Let us reflect upon Harding's three models of action which are a good basis to reflect upon different sorts of responsibility. (Harding 2007, 81–82).

1. Human Individual Action. This is simplest to understand and is appropriate to "interpersonal relations, when the individual's identity as such is a governing dynamic" (Harding 2007, 81).
2. Individuals Acting Collectively as a Group. Harding establishes how this model can demonstrate individuals can both be part of a group and yet, nonetheless, their own "identity as individuals remains a significant determinant of the collective action" (Harding 2007, 82). Here Harding suggests that such reasoning may come into play in

cases of conspiracy. The interesting feature of this model is that it maintains "… (T)hat despite the group context and an important sense of collective enterprise, individual identity and autonomy remain decisive, so that any resulting responsibility for the action in question is seen as a collection of individual responsibilities" (Harding 2007, 82).

3. Corporate Identity. This model takes for granted the reality of the corporate actor and his, or her, agency over and against the agency of flesh and blood persons, *per se*. In this model, responsibility "… would vest in the collective or organisational agent, and not in any associated individuals" (Harding 2007, 82).

Harding's typology is helpful because it is a simple scheme and seems to cohere with our practical reflections. It is easy to see, however, that establishing corporate identity is undoubtedly the most problematic of the models to establish. The second model, individuals acting collectively as a group, seems to be the less contentious. This would be mistaken in very many circumstances. It is worth quoting McDonald here, who Harding also cites:

> Not only does the organisation have all the capacities that are standardly taken to ground autonomy – viz., capacities for intelligent agency – but it also has them to a degree no human can. Thus, for example, a large corporation has available and can make us of more information than one individual can. Moreover, the corporation is in principle 'immortal' and so better able to bear responsibility for its deeds than humans, whose sin dies with them. (McDonald 1987, 219–220)

Other scholars too have argued that in many ways the corporation may indeed be the "paradigm responsible actor" (Fisse and Braithwaite 1993, 30–31; Harding 2007, 86).

Let us look a little closer into the issue of responsibility in terms of its collective and corporate guises. When we decide upon responsibility in cases involving more than a single actor, and notably in relation to organisations, there may be a tendency to use Harding's second model, individuals acting collectively as a group, since it seemingly balances two sets of claims; those relating to individuals acting collectively and those of the organisation, *qua* organisation. In his seminal, *Doing and Deserving*, Joel Feinberg gives us cause to uphold Harding's second model, despite the problem of vicarious liability in which individuals, through no action of their own, are deemed liable for the action of the collective (Morgan 2017, 202–205). This may seem unfair but Feinberg sees things differently:

> Collective liability, as I shall use the term, is the vicarious liability of an organized group (either loosely organized or impermanent collection or a corporate institution) for the actions of its constituent members (Lederman 2000, 651–655). Under certain circumstances, collective liability is a natural and prudent way of arranging the affairs of an organization, which the members might well be expected to undertake themselves, quite voluntarily. This expectation applies only to those organizations (usually small ones) where there is already a high degree of de facto solidarity. (Feinberg 1970, 233)

Interestingly, Feinberg argues that this version of individuals acting collectively as a group has the added benefit of being able to rely, and even buttress, a sense of collective solidarity (Feinberg 1970, 239). Indeed, Feinberg goes so far as to advocate this on the basis of kinship (Gadirov 2013). I object to the wrongfulness of vicarious liability but more so in terms of it violating notions of individual fairness than in relation to matters of kinship; though there too the objection is obvious and easily sustained. You surely cannot be responsible for what you had no control over. Provided vicarious liability is dismissed as a reasonable option the better option is, surely, to hold that indeed members of the collective may be individually responsible in terms of their actions, which could be said to express the internal decision making of the organisation. Harding has argued that conspiracy is a good example of this (Harding 2007, 82). In a case of conspiracy an individual is party to collective responsibility through his, or her, involvement with a collective action. The complicity to conspiracy itself presents the case of responsibility, in this instance, though the conspiracy is separate from the criminal liabilities it establishes in the parties to it. In any case, the level of responsibility of any person in a collective action, where vicarious liability is set aside, must be proportional to their contribution to it. This is, in turn, problematic since establishing that is also rather difficult to do and can probably never be done with total certainty, as Squires has recently shown (Squires 2016).

When we shift from thinking in terms, to a greater or lesser extent, of persons to thinking solely in terms of *organisational* responsibility and *organisational* agency things are rather different; and far more contested at the technical level. For many, the whole idea of any sort of corporate criminal liability is little more than a legal fiction, something to keep the directors of companies out of prison and to put the blame on an abstraction, a legal construction, the organisation. The organisation may exist in law though it is not itself a person in the flesh and blood sense. Wells sees it in many ways as simply enabling organisational agency to step in, *deus ex machina*, and thereby remove many of the questions we might wish to raise in respect to human agency (Wells 2001, 70–81). This, I think, is too strong and that it is quite possible to think of organisations as even fulfilling most of the conditions we might wish to place upon any responsible subject; in other words an organisation may have a stable underlying structure and a distinct role, the capacity to act autonomously and some sense of internal decision making. This being the case, in many instances the organisational subject is absolutely the most appropriate one to hold against a legal standard of responsibility. A good example might well be corporate manslaughter, rather than trying to attribute blame to persons operating, themselves, within an organisational structure; and such cases are regularly brought before the courts. Whilst using the device of the corporate subject is often contentious in relation to private companies when it is related to the person of the state there is far less disagreement amongst citizens, lawyers and scholars (Cassese 2005). In both legal and political theory, in addition to statute law, it is universally accepted in international law that the state is not only real but is both the source of ultimate volition and what we might term the primary responsible agent. Moreover, the state also gives rights, and laws, as well as also being bound by them and in this way is a rather special subject (Amatrudo and Blake 2015; Brownlie 2003). One important point to note here, however, is that whilst it is undoubtedly the case that the state is taken as a responsible subject in law, there is widespread dispute as to whether, or not, this falls short of moral responsibility, in the classical sense; and which Hart located in the human subject alone (Hart 1968). The currently dominant realist view tends to assert that the organisation can be said to simply exist, in time, as a distinct entity and that all the law does is to substantiate and demarcate this already established existence (Ferran 1999).

Hart on Responsibility

Organisations, like individuals, may be held legally accountable for their actions. They are responsible in law, responsibility being understood as simply the mechanism used for allotting subjects into a normative framework based on their prior actions. Where the matter of obligation arises, such as in relation to agreed standards of behaviour, again responsibility is the mechanism by which we typically judge the significance of failing to satisfy those obligations. In this way, subjects and obligations are linked. The most well-known elaboration of responsibility was furnished by H.L.A. Hart in which he sets out four exemplars of responsibility. Hart's work still remains the classic statement of responsibility and very useful to our discussions in that he deals with both the subject's objective place in an organisation, by means of role responsibility, and the subject's agency through his notion of causal responsibility which connects the subject's actions with events. Hart's sense of what he termed "liability responsibility" will be shown to be important in terms of determining responsibility, in each case, and thereafter the level of appropriate sanction. In any case, Hart's normative approach, moreover, has been enormously influential beyond the world of legal scholarship and has been taken up by political theorists and public policy thinkers too. It is useful here to set out Hart's model by way of a simple formula. In Hart, we note:

$$(A+B) \times C = R$$

Where A = role; B = capacity; C = the case in question; and R = the appropriate level of criminal responsibility.

In Hart's model, criminal responsibility is simply the appropriate level of response to a given issue that impinges upon civic order and solidarity. Hart's four types of responsibility (role responsibility, causal responsibility, liability responsibility and capacity responsibility) we can reason by means of simple exemplars.

(1) As the driver of the train I am responsible for ensuring passenger safety.
(2) As the person who stabbed and murdered Sarah I caused her death and am responsible for it.
(3) As Jennifer's manager, I have a managerial function around her employment and so am legally liable for any problems Jennifer's employment causes.
(4) Since I am a rational and autonomous person I am responsible for my own actions. I should therefore be held accountable for how I behave.

These four senses in Hart's taxonomy elegantly set out the numerous psychological and sociological processes at work when determining responsibility (Hart 1968, 265). Liability responsibility is, though, definitely afforded priority by Hart since it is the final stage, dependent upon the others. It establishes the importance of capacity and role, as both being prior to liability responsibility and establishing the basis for liability responsibility (Hart 1968, 224–225). Liability responsibility is merely the outcome of the ontological realities of capacity and role. At the outset, there needs initially to be a social association made between the subject and the actions they perform in relation to the obligation at issue. Role responsibility is basically concerned with a place or office in an organisation; and this is not a very easy thing to always establish. My example, of the train driver, is clear enough but accounting for responsibility in, say, a power station or similar engineering context or any manner of complex organisation seems much more difficult. Hart himself acknowledged this (Hart 1968, 212). Moreover, my example of the train driver is possibly too strong and that some responsibility will doubtless rest with maintenance staff, conductors and a host of others who also have a role in the operation of the train; to say nothing of the management not on the ground, shareholders and designated safety officials. We note, at least, how the matter of responsibility even in a seemingly straightforward case is likely to be more complicated than an initial reflection might result in and the grounds for contestation very wide. The methodology seems reasonable enough but the practical task is obviously more involved, the more so given the disaggregation of functions. We can hold, nonetheless, that determining responsibility is essentially a matter about roles and how to define those roles: and asking whether, or not, subjects may be placed in a designated role. Importantly, this matter of role responsibility ultimately determines the limits of a subject's responsibility and lays the ground for, what Hart termed, "capacity responsibility" which determines those psychological and intellectual, moral if you like, capacities that form the internal landscape of any responsible subject.

In his notion of capacity responsibility, Hart shows that for any role that is undertaken the subject must possess some capacity to understand how the role they perform can generate consequences. It is important too in establishing the subject's *mens rea* in their decision-making processes and without this innate capacity the whole notion of responsibility is rather compromised. Hart expresses this neatly:

> (Those) crimes carrying severe penalties, is made by law to depend … on certain mental conditions … the individual is not liable to punishment if at the time of his doing what would otherwise be a punishable act he was unconscious, mistaken about the physical consequences of his bodily movements or the nature or qualities of the thing or persons affected by them, or, in some cases, if he was subjected to threats or other gross forms of coercion or was the victim of certain types of mental disease. (Hart 1968, 81)

The statement I supply here, by Hart, does rather rest on a *human* subjectivity being in question and not a *corporate* one. Of course, this has often been raised by way of objection to corporate responsibility. We can, however, argue that the decision-making structures of organisations, though non-human, exhibit a version of rationality nonetheless. Moreover, one may posit that the corporate subject may very well be thought of as both separate from its human elements and be held separately responsible.

This is most readily seen in relation to so-called delinquent organisations whose organisational culture and decision making may not be attributed to human subjects who are part of the corporate structure: moreover, where such a delinquent organisational culture and decision making are established they, surely, form the basis of corporate responsibility. In this case, it is obvious that such reasoning suits the action of states, whose role, agency capacity, is readily apparent. The useful thing, for our purposes, is the claim that responsibility can be established by showing how responsibility (i.e. the principle of responsibility) may be established when there is a rupture between the role and capacity of a subject and the norm of behaviour. Hart's causal responsibility moves from establishing roles and capacities to liabilities for punishment or sanction.

Hart's causal responsibility provides the necessary pre-condition for moral appraisal and legal liability and is the *condition sine qua non* of the empirical nature of any conclusions reached. We must not think it a simple matter relating to events. Causation is rarely a simple matter in criminal law though, unfortunately, some legal scholars often maintain that it is (Simester and Sullivan 2003, 88; Harding 2007, 110–111). Alan Norrie, in discussing the 1981 Brixton Riots, noted how deeper and less visible factors such as poor social housing and deep-seated institutional racism also form part of the environment that led up to the rioting. Norrie saw these deeper and less visible factors as part and parcel of everyday life for residents and he bemoaned them being excluded from the enterprise of determining the causation for the riots too (Norrie 1991, 685–692). Norrie is right to flag up how deeper and less visible factors are often part of the causal explanation and not simply the matter at hand. It seems also to say something about a writer's politics: critical writers, such as Norrie, looking to deeper and less visible factors and others who note only the immediate, and visible, saying something too about their own notions of law, values and world-view. The point Norrie makes is archetypal and divides writers across disciplines.

The distinction we draw between Hart's first three types of responsibility (role, capacity and cause) and his last (liability) is simply that the first three need determining and categorising; whereas, the fourth establishes the responsibility (i.e. liability) in each case and, it follows, the appropriate level of sanction. If you like, role, capacity and cause *serve* liability, in the sense, that they provide the grounds for it. Liability is then, the out-come of the initial three types of responsibility i.e. role, capacity and cause (Hart 1968, 215–228). Obviously, different forms of agency, different sorts of subjects; and different sorts of subjects give rise to a range of appropriate liabilities. The determination of responsibility is crucially about holding a subject responsible for their actions in the setting of the legal domain where liability is attributed. Liability, in this sense, is the ultimate demonstration of responsibility. It will be expressed, usually, formally by way of legal judgment; and it will, usually, be backed up through the imposition of a sanction which may be said to communicate the level of responsibility breached. It will, usually, support the existing moral world-view of the society it takes place in. Ratner has put this in a very broad context when he, rather optimistically, writes: "Nonetheless, the law can, as it does in countless other areas … offer a common language in this debate, as well as a set of standards that can be enforced. The duties resulting when these actors work through the above theory will clearly satisfy no group fully. But if prescribed and applied by legitimate and effective institutions, or enforced … these norms represent the beginning of a more global and coherent response to new challenges to human dignity" (Ratner 2001, 452).

Accounting for the Criminal Elements of Liability and Responsibility

The determination of liability is the ultimate expression of responsibility. As we noted earlier, it is generally formal and generally involves some form of sanction. The sanction being the rightful expression of a rightful determination of liability (von Hirsch 1996). This is typically the case when the law is concerned though not always and legal cases may increase, or decrease, tariffs to express the considered view of society, at that time, or involve a utilitarian calculus which may result in a noted disproportionality. It is also the case that in legal cases the sanction imposed may take the form of damages, injunctions in the form of banning, exclusion or prohibition orders, and/or the seizure of assets; we should not always think in terms of imprisonment as a sanction. The determination of what sanction is appropriate will be tailored to the individual case but will always be in terms of, what I term, *expressive* rectification. In other words, in its legal form, the sanction is largely categorised by the expression, by way of a censure (Amatrudo 2017). Importantly, the level of the sanction does reflect the level of censure and that there is a sense of proportionality at work.

A Word on Proportionality

The main thrust of modern, recent, retributive thinking on the topic of proportionality is that it should gauge moral seriousness. It follows from this that serious crimes ought to incur a harsher penalty than less serious ones. Moreover, that this should be the only gauge. This principle is hardly new as Bentham wrote: "The greater the mischief of the offence, the greater the expense, which it may be worthwhile to be at, in the way of punishment" (Bentham 1982, 168). In recent retributivist writing, such as just desert theory, moral seriousness is ascertained by looking at two variables: (1) the harm done by the offence and (2) the culpability of the offender (Bedau 1978; von Hirsch 1978). There have been scholars and jurists who advocated for punishment to be justified purely in terms of its consequences; in terms of, for example, rehabilitation or crime prevention. There have been those who argued that though punishment may have long, and emotional, roots that it is has a primary utility in strengthening existing social bonds (Mackie 1985). In other words, punishment has utility due to its consequentialist rationale. Andreas von Hirsch, on the other hand, maintained that it: "(F)ails adequately to support ethical limits on the distribution of sanctions" (von Hirsch 1990, 407–409). The problem being that since Mackie overlooked the matter of the distribution of sanctions, the possibility arises of disproportionate punishments and criminal liability without fault. Hart reasoned that relying on crime prevention as the general justifying aim of punishment, however, may leave space for putting non-utilitarian limits on the distribution of penalties, but only when the latter can be independently justified (Hart 1968). Hart argued that there must be an independent justification for a retributive limit on substantive Criminal Law, since liability must be confined to the culpability of the criminal in question (Hart 1968, 112). Hart's position is derived from his prioritising of the ideals of choice and freedom of action. A free society must make it possible for persons to conduct a good and crime-free life. They ought, by good living, be able to avoid the sanctions of the Criminal Law, and this can only be facilitated when the Criminal Law operates through a system of strict criminal liability. Otherwise, simple accidental breaches could render persons criminally liabile. Hart's justification has some issues in terms of sentencing policy and when matters of proportionality are addressed where we hold that punishments must always be proportionate to the level of seriousness of the crime. In which case, proportionality may not be anchored in some value, like equal opportunity, to avoid punishment because it relates solely to those persons who, of their own will, have chosen to break the law, and who, therefore, are subject to criminal liability. Hart's view was that without proportionality our common morality would disintegrate and that, over time, the law would come to be held in contempt. Hart's view is, however, a rather weak justification for proportionality. The notion that society must maintain a common morality is also a utilitarian consideration and on that basis open to being set aside, as when the law is held in contempt. Hart's defence of proportionality seems too weak and must be excluded.

Censure may offer strong justifying reasons for adopting a non-utilitarian rationale for proportionality, consistent with a consequentialist general justifying aim, nonetheless. We take for granted that crime is censured even in cases where the general justifying aim is crime prevention; the sanction always being expressed in terms of how blameworthy it was. Moreover, we may reason that when proportionality is not followed then it is criminals, above all, who are wrongly treated (von Hirsch 1985, 34–36). Criminal sanctions may well have some preventive impact but determining whether this derives, and to what degree, from the application of a sanction on a person, or set of persons, is unlikely to ever be established with a great deal of accuracy. If, of course, we decide that censure is not necessary in terms of crime prevention then this is no longer an issue. It is, surely, possible to advocate for a consequentialist justification of punishment and remain wedded to proportionality. This position is often attributed to Kant but this, according to Murphy, is to unhelpfully oversimplify the matter (Murphy 1987, 509). This view, now arguably the dominant view, came about through a discussion between philosophers, and legal theorists in the late 1960s and on through the 1980s, beginning with Morris's seminal 1968 article "Persons and Punishment" (Finnis 1980; Gerwirth 1978; Morris 1968, 475–501; Murphy 1987; Sadurski 1985).

This position is termed the benefits and burdens approach and accounts for why criminals must suffer. It understands the criminal law as having two main functions. The law demands that every person refrains from committing crime and in so doing benefit from the restraint of other people. Anyone who undertakes criminal activity is understood as, unfairly, benefitting from the self-restraint of their fellows and thus seeks to obtain an unfair advantage. The criminal sanction is that institution which imposes upon the criminal some form of objective disadvantage, so as to restore what we might term the balance of advantages, as between persons. This position came under attack from von Hirsch in *Doing Justice*, and later by Duff in *Trials and Punishment* (Duff 1986). The principal problem that von Hirsch and Duff understood was that even if a balance of advantages is achieved it may be insufficient to invoke the state power that may be required. Moreover, as von Hirsch argued in *Past or Future Crimes?*, this benefits and burdens view of retributivism also, somewhat, implies an expansive contractarian theory of the state (von Hirsch 1985; Davis 1983).

Civil and Criminal Matters in Criminal Responsibility

There is the matter of what sanctions to choose and how to classify them, as between civil and criminal. This is sometimes a complex determination and often a breach gives rise to either sort of sanction, or indeed, both. It is not uncommon to impose a criminal sanction and, for example, a compensation order. Moreover, the decision regarding whether to apply civil or criminal sanctions may also be related to the symbolic nature of the sanction above all else. Typically, criminal sanctions imply a greater level of censure (Fisse and Braithwaite 1993). The criminal sanction also implies a much greater level of seriousness, in terms of the breach in question, *vis-à-vis* social cohesion and public order. As Harding has noted: "Overall, it is difficult to escape the sense of the civil-criminal dichotomy as fundamental for purposes of categorizing in an expressive way the nature of legal responsibility (Harding 2007, 117).

Criminal Responsibility and Organisational Actors

Since this topic is so vast we will confine our discussion to the core issues of criminal enterprise as it relates to the criminal organisation. We may think of the criminal organisation as another type of organisational actor that may be held responsible for its actions legally, and distinctly from its constituent members. We hold that typically organisations commit different sorts of crimes from their constituent members; and we further note that this recognises that there are justified limits to the extent of responsibility to which we may hold individual persons. It is clearly established in law that the corporate (i.e. relating to a body or organisation) criminal exists at a broad level but as the determination gets narrower there is a tendency to hold individuals responsible. In any case, such determinations are often marked by a lack of clarity in terms of how to establish the limits of individual responsibility and by a great deal of controversy whenever a determination is made (Lederman 2000). The issue is how to prove a separate form of organisational agency; separate that is from the agency of individuals within it. This will mean establishing a distinct organisational form of rationality. It will also entail convincingly showing that, if not completely immaterial, the agency of individual persons is of less importance than the agency of the organisation, *qua* agency (Jeßberger 2016). Lastly, it will need to be demonstrated that the organisation had a free and self-sufficient capacity for action, of its own. Lederman has argued:

> ... (That) a new socio-political-economic reality, characterized by a thriving common market in Europe, changes in the political regimes of Eastern

Europe, intensive privatization processes in many countries that shifted many areas of activity to the non-governmental sector, and the creation of mega-multinational-corporations that are the result of acquisitions, mergers and takeovers. In a process that peaked in the second half of this century, legal bodies have assumed control of all forms of commerce and industry, to the extent that no economic endeavour is deemed possible without their involvement. This socio-economic reality has dictated, to a large extent, the change in the law's approach to the imposition of penal liability on corporations. Policy setters in various legislative and law enforcement bodies sensed that attaining effective, and mainly trouble-free, control of the economy through criminal law depends on a sweeping subordination of the legal bodies themselves, as far as possible, to criminal proceedings. All this without restricting the scope of the personal criminal liability incumbent on management ranks or on those actually involved in breaking law. (Lederman 2000, 644)

The core issue is the determination of organisational rationality to undertake action and to display internal decision making beyond the mere aggregation of individual persons and their contributions. This sort of reasoning is well-attested to in the philosophical literature and a typical defence of a non-individualistic account runs along the following lines: though the rationality of an organisation may start off with individual contributions from individual persons these arise out of human interaction, which is different in nature in relation to the form of rationality that an organisation displays, and that interaction is not coterminous with contribution; and that interaction may transform these elements, via the workings of human culture, into a form of life wherein the determining factor in the interaction is the organisation, not the individual. The corporate replaces the sum of the parts. Arnold puts this well: "As with shared intentions, corporate intentions are neither a set of individual mental states, nor the mental state of some super-agent. Corporate intentions are states of affairs consisting of both the intersecting attitudes of the class of agents comprising the corporation and the internal decision structure of the organization" (Arnold 2006, 291).

The claim that the agency of individual persons is of little consequence is an idea that was developed initially by Coleman in his 1982

The Asymmetric Society: Organizational Actors, Corporate Power and the Irrelevance of Persons. Coleman sought to show the individual marginal importance of individuals in an organisation. He did this by using a well-established sociological distinction between persons and their roles. Coleman asserts that it is often the case that in many ways the role is of more importance than the person when accounting for how individuals are to be thought of in terms of corporate responsibility. The long-standing organisational structure is both to, and enduring after, the individual. The organisation has a form of reasoning that is beyond the outcome of individuals. It might be added here that echoes of this sort of reasoning are given by Luhmann and his systems theory approach, within sociological theory (Luhmann 1984). One notes how, if we follow the Coleman–Luhmann approach, that it is only a short step from conceiving of the organisation as having the capacity for free, and self-sufficient, action, of its own, based on its self-sufficient decision-making ability. It will possess, after all, the necessary structure, identity and role to be self-sufficient. It is, of course, possible to interact with the organisation, not as an aggregation of persons, but as an actor itself. It will possess a role related to its purpose and therefore a separate identity based on its capacity for independent action, or if you like, agency. Moreover, its capacity for independent action dispenses with the need for it to have a flesh and blood doppelganger and undercuts the criticism of anthropomorphism.

In developing an argument for corporate organisational responsibility, we necessarily realise the limitations upon the responsibility of individual persons; and an analysis that realises this can discern wrongdoing in terms of organisational culture that is much more serious than at the atomised level of the individual actor: such as a form of corporate greed which prioritises profit over, for example, health and safety considerations (Slapper and Tombs 1999). In such cases, it is obviously the right thing to pursue the organisation as the primary bearer of responsibility. It is easy to see how it may be more straightforward, given what we have established about organisational actors, to seek criminal liability at the corporate level, in the first instance (Tombs and Whyte 2015).

Criminal Enterprise As an Organisational Rationale

We should note, at this point, that having established the basis for organisational criminal responsibility that it can loop back, as it were, to underpin personal responsibility too. The organisation serves as the anchoring point for individual criminal activity. We see this especially in relation to the treatment of members of proscribed Nazi organisations where the organisation was set up as a criminal enterprise. Here I have in mind the scholarship of Hilary Earl and her painstaking research into the SS-Einsatzgruppen Trial, following the Second World War, where participatory individual responsibility was established by reference to the organisation, as *delinquent* criminal enterprise (Earl 2009, 2013b). The issue at hand in the SS-Einsatzgruppen Trial was essentially one of involvement in a sort of common criminal enterprise and involvement in the structures of that common criminal enterprise. Cassese, writing more generally, has argued that:

> All participants in a common criminal action are equally responsible, if they (1) participate in the action, *whatever their position and the extent of their contribution*, and in addition (2) *intend to engage in the common criminal action*. Therefore, they are all treated as *principals*, although of course the varying degree of culpability may be taken into account at the sentencing stage .... (1) each of them is indispensable for the achievement of the final result, and on the other hand, (2) it would be difficult to distinguish between the degree of criminal liability, except for sentencing. (Cassese 2003, 181–182)

These are the grounds for joint criminal enterprise on which is built joint criminal liability and its ontological basis distinguishes it from a conspiracy (Sergi 2014). The essential point to grasp here is simply that in the cases that we have in mind it is the sheer complexity of the organisations in question that is an issue. Therefore, it is usually straightforward to look at individuals in a disaggregated way and hold them liable for their discrete activity. However, that can leave the greater crimes, of the organisation, unchallenged. Moreover, disaggregation seems to entirely miss what we might call the *facilitating* capacity of the organisation. It is unlikely individuals would have committed their individual crimes if this were not the case (Earl 2009, 96–134). The organisation often brings about a situation wherein individuals may commit crime and this must be admitted. The organisation gives individuals a sense of purpose. The label we give to this sort of situation we term joint enterprise or common purpose, or some such. These terms attempt to capture a sense of the individual interacting and participating in the structure of the organisation: in which case, all those who take part in a joint enterprise are equally responsible. They share the responsibility *jointly* (Sanchez-Brigado 2010, 141–161). Organisations may have delinquent objectives which structure activity so as to give rise to discrete criminal activity but this is not conspiracy rather it is better understood in terms of Cassese's ideas about organisational acts that often seem pedestrian, not obviously criminal, more bureaucratic than anything else (Cassese 2003, 182–183). Moreover, organisational structures and the remoteness of senior persons from day-to-day matters can militate against a successful prosecution. The example, that is revisited time after time is that of Adolf Eichmann, the SS-Lieutenant Colonel who ran Department IV B4 of the RSHA (Reich Main Security Office) that oversaw Jewish affairs and deportations of Jews. Eichmann attended the infamous 1942 Wannsee Conference of senior Nazis convened by Reinhard Heydrich that determined the coordination and administrative systems for the so-called *Final Solution to the Jewish Question* which sought to deport all the Jews of Nazi-occupied Europe to be systematically murdered in camps, mainly in Poland. Eichmann was not so much involved with policy but with the operational outcomes dictated by his superiors (Cesarani 2005). At Wannsee, Eichmann served as the official note-taker. Eichmann was captured in Argentina by Mossad agents and tried in Jerusalem after escaping Germany after the Second World War. He argued at his trial that there was an over-concentration upon his coordinating role in the Holocaust rather than that of others who committed the murders. This completely missed the joint enterprise principle which stipulates the importance of the overall structure of the collective, including the role of facilitation. It was Eichmann's role that led to the offences of murder committed by others. In the Holocaust, we have the example of many people coming together to commit a huge crime, or series of crimes, not in terms of a conspiracy but as part of an organisation. It follows then that the criminal structure, i.e. the organisation, becomes the important actor (along with the policies and directives that motivate it). In the first count taken at the Nuremberg Trial this is acknowledged with its language of a *common plan* to commit crimes, though it also used the term *conspiracy* (Bush 2017). We note how joint enterprise crime, which concerns crimes of participation, can easily, through sloppy drafting or lack of focus on the part of prosecutors, get intertwined with crimes of membership, conspiracy or predicate offending (i.e. a crime that is a component, or sub-set, of a larger criminal offence. Moreover, membership (e.g. of a criminal organisation such as the Gestapo, the Mafia, the IRA) can be indicative of the criminal activity of, and on behalf of, the delinquent organisation in question. The important point is that in joint enterprise there is a sharing of responsibility between the organisation and the individuals that make it up: but there is room to differentiate the actions, and amount of responsibility, between actors. It also matters whether, or not, actors are aware of their liability and therefore responsibility for undertaking different actions (Cassese 2003, 145). One of the issues with the Holocaust is that it is such a huge crime and involved so many—persons, bureaucrats, railway drivers, doctors, soldiers, police officers and at one level the entire nation—that it is difficult to specify the level of liability of each and every person involved in it. Yet we want to hold that this is possible; certainly at the level of those actively working in the camps or in the killing squads. The point remains, however, that those actively working in the camps or in the killing squads were, in turn, supported by others: many of whom were well-aware of their facilitating role (Anderson 1994).

In conclusion, I think there is certainly merit in thinking of organisations as having agency, or agency they share with individuals. However, for organisations to function in this fashion they need to persist in time and, as we saw earlier, to exhibit (1) a stable underlying structure and (2) some sense of internal decision making. These two important provisos seem to compromise, in very many cases, applying the notion of criminal enterprise to looser groupings, such as street gangs, who cannot meet those criteria (as we saw in Chaps. 1 and 2). Agency certainly has a role in more formal, stable and self-willing organisations, such as with proscribed Nazi organisations like the SS-Einsatzgruppen or organised white-collar crime and the like where a stable underlying structure and a sense of internal decision-making are more apparent (Sanchez-Brigado 2010, 163–185). The debate ensues where (1) a stable underlying structure and (2) some sense of internal decision making is disputed.

Bibliography

Amatrudo, A. (2017). *Social Censure and Critical Criminology: After Sumner*. Basingstoke: Palgrave Macmillan.

Amatrudo, A., & Blake, L. (2015). *Human Rights and the Criminal Justice System*. London: Routledge.

Anderson, K. (1994). Nuremberg Sensibility. *Harvard Human Rights Journal, 7*(3), 281–295.

Arnold, D. (2006). Corporate Moral Agency. *Midwest Studies in Philosophy, 30*(1), 279–291.

Bedau, H. A. (1978). Retribution and the Theory of Punishment. *Journal of Philosophy, 75*(2), 601–620.

Bentham. J. (1982). In J. H. Burns & H. L. A. Hart (Eds.), *An Introduction to the Principles of Morals and Legislation*. London: Methuen.

Blickle, G., Schlegel, A., Fassbender, P., & Klein, U. (2006). Some Personality Correlates of Business White-Collar Crime. *Applied Psychology: An International Review, 55*(2), 220–223.

Brownlie, I. (2003). *Principles of Public International Law*. Oxford: OUP.

Bush, J. (2017). Nuremberg and Beyond. *Loyola LA International and Comparative Law Review, 259*(39), 259–286.

Cassese, A. (2003). *International Criminal Law*. Oxford: OUP.

Cassese, A. (2005). *International Law*. Oxford: OUP.

Cesarani, D. (2005). *Eichmann: His Life and Crimes*. London: Vintage.

Dan-Cohen, M. (1994). Between Selves and Collectivities: Towards a Jurisprudence of Identity. *University of Chicago Law Review, 61*(4), 1213–1243.

Davis, M. (1983). How to Make the Punishment Fit the Crime. *Ethics, 93*(2), 726–752.

Duff, R. A. (1986). *Trials and Punishment*. Cambridge: Cambridge University Press.

Earl, H. (2009). *The Nuremberg SS-Einsatzgruppen Trial, 1945–1958: Atrocity Law and History*. New York: Cambridge University Press.

Earl, H. (2013a). Prosecuting Genocide Before the Genocide Convention: Raphael Lemkin and the Nuremberg Trials, 1945–1949. *Journal of Genocide Research, 15*(3), 317–338.

Earl, H. (2013b). Beweise, Zeugen, Narrative: Der Einsatzgruppen Prozess und seine Wirkung auf die historische Forschung zur Genese der Endlösung. In K. C. Priemel & A. Stiller (Eds.), *NMT. Nürnberger Militärtribunale zwischen Geschichte, Gerechigkeit und Rechtschöpfung* (pp. 127–157). Springer.

Erskine, T. (2003). *Can Institutions Have Responsibilities?* Basingstoke: Palgrave Macmillan.

Feinberg, J. (1970). *Doing and Deserving*. Princeton: Princeton University Press.

Ferran, E. (1999). *Company Law and Corporate Finance*. Oxford: OUP.

Finnis, F. (1980). *Natural Law and Natural Rights*. Oxford: Clarendon Press.

Fisse, B., & Braithwaite, J. (1993). *Corporations, Crime and Accountability*. Cambridge: Cambridge University Press.

Gadirov, J. (2013). Casual Responsibility International Criminal Law. *International Criminal Law Review, 15*(5), 970–987.

Gerwirth, A. (1978). *Reason and Morality*. Chicago: Chicago University Press.

Gowa, J., & Mansfield, E. (2004). Alliances, Imperfect Markets and Major-Power Trade. *International Organisation, 58*(2), 775–805.

Gupta, A., Briscoe, F., & Hambrick, D. (2017). Red, Blue, and Purple Firms: Organizational Political Ideology and Corporate Social Responsibility. *Strategic Management Journal, 38*(5), 1018–1040.

Harding, C. (2007). *Criminal Enterprise: Individuals, Organisations and Criminal Responsibility*. Cullompton: Willan Press.

Hart, H. L. A. (1968). *Punishment and Responsibility: Essays in the Philosophy of Law*. Oxford: OUP.

von Hirsch, A. (1978). Proportionality and Desert: A Reply to Bedau. *Journal of Philosophy, 75*(2), 622–624.

von Hirsch, A. (1985). *Past or Future Crimes?* Manchester: Manchester University Press.

von Hirsch, A. (1990). The Politics of Just Deserts. *Canadian Journal of Criminology, 397*(32), 407–409.

von Hirsch, A. (1996). *Censure and Sanctions*. Oxford: Clarendon Press.

Jeßberger, F. (2016). Corporate Involvement in Slavery and Criminal Responsibility Under International Law. *Journal of International Criminal Justice, 14*(2), 327–341.

Kelsen, H. (1999). *General Theory of Law and State*. Cambridge: Harvard University Press.

Lederman, E. (2000). Models for Imposing Corporate Criminal Liability: From Adoption and Imitation Towards Aggregation and the Search for Self-Identity. *Buffalo Criminal Law Review, 4*(1), 641–708.

List, C., & Petit, P. (2011). *Group Agency: The Possibility, Design and Status of Corporate Agents*. Oxford: OUP.

Luhmann, N. (1984). *Soziale Systeme: Grundriß einer allgemeinen Theorie*. Frankfurt: Suhrkamp.

Mackie, J. L. (1985). *Persons and Values*. Oxford: Clarendon Press.

McDonald, M. (1987). The Personless Paradigm. *University of Toronto Law Journal, 37*(212), 219–220.

Morgan, P. (2017). Certainty in Vicarious Liability: A Quest for a Chimera? *Cambridge Law Journal, 75*(2), 202–205.

Morris, H. (1968). Persons and Punishment. *The Monist, 52*(4), 475–501.

Murphy, J. (1987). Does Kant Have a Theory of Punishment? *Columbia Law Review, 87*(3), 509–542.

Norrie, A. (1991). A Critique of Criminal Causation. *Modern Law Review, 54*(5), 685–701.

Pontell, H., Black, N., William, K., & Geis, G. (2014). Too Big to Fail, Too Powerful to Jail? On the Absence of Criminal Prosecutions after the 2008 Financial Meltdown. *Crime, Law and Social Change, 61*(1), 1–13.

Ratner, S. (2001). Corporations and Human Rights; A Theory of Legal Responsibility. *Yale Law Journal, 111*(93), 443–545.

Sadurski, W. (1985). *Giving Desert Its Due*. Lancaster/Dordrecht: Springer.

Sanchez-Brigado, R. E. (2010). *Groups, Rules and Legal Practice*. London: Springer.

Sergi, A. (2014). Organised Crime in Criminal Law: Conspiracy and Membership Offences in Italian, English and International Frameworks. *Kings Law Journal, 25*(2), 185–200.

Simester, A., & Sullivan, G. (2003). *Criminal Law: Theory and Doctrine*. Oxford: Hart.

Slapper, G., & Tombs, S. (1999). *Corporate Crime*. London: Longman.

Squires, P. (2016). *Voodoo Liability*: Joint Enterprise Prosecution as an Aspect of Intensified Criminalisation. *The Politics and Jurisprudence of Group Offending: Onati Socio-Legal Series, 6*(4), 937–956.

Tombs, S., & Whyte, D. (2015). Counterblast: Crime, Harm and the State-Corporate Nexus. *Howard Journal of Criminal Justice, 54*(1), 91–95.

Tosun, J., Koos, S., & Shore, J. (2016). Co-governing Common Goods: Interaction Patterns of Private and Public Actors. *Policy and Society, 35*(1), 1–12.
Wells, C. (2001). *Corporations and Criminal Responsibility*. Oxford: OUP.

Section 3

Reality and Sociology

5

Real-Life Cases: War Criminal Prosecutions and the Treatment of Membership of Illegal Organisations

Any work that deals with criminal actions and social situations will have to, at some point, get down to the task of looking at real-world examples. Accordingly, we shall focus on two examples: (1) war crimes, concentrating especially upon crimes of the Nazis, notably the SS-Einsatzgruppen Trial, and (2) membership of illegal, or criminal, organisations, in other words those proscribed by law, but more particularly those organisations which assume *responsibility*, in group offending cases, where individual responsibility ends. We shall look at terrorist groups and the SS-Einsatzgruppen, by way of an example. The model for these two examples, in terms of collective intentional action, will follow on from Sanchez-Brigado who advanced the following model:

a. each conceives of a state of affairs the bringing about of which involves, or is constituted by, the performance of certain actions (and the display of certain attitudes) by all members of the set;
b. their conceptions of this state of affairs overlap;
c. each intends to perform these actions (and attitudes) as related in the way described to the state of affairs;
d. and each executes his or her intention, such that the state of affairs mentioned in (b) obtains (Sanchez-Brigado 2010, 85).

© The Author(s) 2018
A. Amatrudo, *Criminal Actions and Social Situations*,
https://doi.org/10.1057/978-1-137-45731-8_5

In following Sanchez-Brigado we capture the individual responsibility of persons and note how the organisation both constitutes and facilitates actions and attitudes. It is important to think in terms of a strict model, or template, that sets out the core elements of the common nature of the group and says something important about its rationale for being and acting.

SS-Einsatzgruppen Trial

The horrors of the Nazi Holocaust involved thousands of people who supported it through their efforts but amongst the very worst of the direct perpetrators were the SS-Einsatzgruppen. The SS-Einsatzgruppen (best translated as special *operational* groups) were mobile squads of military and paramilitary personnel drawn from the SS and various police forces; all of which fell under the auspices of the Reichssicheitshauptamt (RSHA, Reich Main Security Office) although originally the SS-Einsatzgruppen were controlled by the Sicherheitpolizei (SiPo, Security Police). They were formed as early as 1938 when they were used as mobile squads that supported the military annexation of the Sudetenland and Austria. They coordinated matters on the ground in terms of the rounding up of intellectuals, partisans and Jews in the early days of the Nazi occupation, as well as organising local policing and obtaining intelligence from those they took into custody. The SS-Einsatzgruppen also had a leading role in the Action T4, a Nazi programme that sought to systematically murder the mentally ill and the physically handicapped. They were considered a success and in 1939 further SS-Einsatzgruppen squads were created for the invasion of Poland where they went on to carry out the wholesale murder of Polish intellectuals and military officers (Rossino 2003). The focus of the SS-Einsatzgruppen squads developed, over time, and soon after the new squads were formed in Poland their sole *raison d'etre* became murder, mass-murder. They retained their security and intelligence functions, but only in relation to their role in the murder of Jews and other so-called enemies of the Reich. The emphasis upon mass-murder and the coordination of this with local people became integral to the Nazi battle-plan. By the time of the invasion of the Soviet Union with Operation

Barbarossa in June1941 and the plan to annihilate the Jews of the Soviet Union, mass-murder was their sole operational function. In 1941 the various SS-Einsatzgruppen squads were organised into four groups (A initially led by Walther Stahlecker and later by Heinz Jost; B led by Arthur Nebe and later by Erich Naumann; C led by Otto Rasch; and D led by Otto Ohlendorf) under the control of a senior officer in the SS. After the invasion of the Soviet Union with Operation Barbarossa they were officially assigned to the tactical command of the Wehrmacht, as intelligence gathering and security units, although in truth this was largely to cover their true operational role and they took orders from the Reich Main Security Office in Berlin, under the command of Reinhard Heydrich. The SS-Einsatzgruppen after Operation Barbarossa set about systematically killing the various groups that the Reich Main Security Office in Berlin had determined were enemies of the Reich and this included intellectuals and partisans but also gypsies, the mentally ill and especially the Jews. The way they operated was standardised: after the Wehrmacht had taken a territory and secured it the SS-Einsatzgruppen units were called in to systematically round up, rob and then kill Jews and other so-called enemies of the Reich. Initially the mass-murders were undertaken openly but later the victims were usually taken to wooded areas and other places away from the public. The mass-murders were undertaken with great efficiency but many of the SS-Einsatzgruppen, and other involved in the killings, could not deal with the psychological stress and there were many cases of mental breakdown, alcoholism and self-harm. The sheer brutality of systematically murdering old men, women and children day after day on a huge scale led Himmler to seek less upsetting ways to murder, upsetting for the perpetrators that is. The leadership of the SS, accordingly, sought to develop new, more mechanised, forms of mass-murder (Longerich 2012, 541–574). They did this themselves but they also coordinated others in committing mass-murder: various Wehrmacht, police and auxiliary police and locally recruited militia and auxiliary police units were all coordinated in the mass-murder of Jews, partisan and others by the SS-Einsatzgruppen. An example of this sort of coordination is the infamous 707 Security Division of the Wehrmacht. The 707 Security Division was deployed in the Soviet Union in 1941 and took part in anti-partisan operations, including the murder of Jews (Rutherford 2014).

The SS-Einsatzgruppen had a very close working relationship with the Wehrmacht and with the Romanian Army (Marrus 2000). There were never any more than 3000 members of the SS-Einsatzgruppen spread across a vast area of Central and Eastern Europe and the role they had in supporting others in their heinous work is, arguably, an important part of their role as direct murders. It is certainly the case that there were not enough members of the SS-Einsatzgruppen for them to conduct all the killing themselves.

The work of the SS-Einsatzgruppen was part of a systematic process which was organised by the Reich Main Security Office in Berlin in collaboration with the Wehrmacht operating under the legal mandate of a *Führerbefehl* (Fuhrer-order) relating to the Jews and the invasion of the Soviet Union. There is some dispute as to whether, or not, SS-Einsatzgruppen soldiers were ever formally given the *Führerbefehl* but that is a less important point than the realisation that the Reich Main Security Office in Berlin in collaboration, and the Wehrmacht, at the highest levels of command, certainly were acting on the basis that the mass-murders were supported at the very highest political levels in the Third Reich—and they operated on that basis (Kershaw 2008). Local leaders of the SS-Einsatzgruppen were certainly aware of the *Führerbefehl*, or other superior orders, on the basis that the programme of mass-murder was supported at the highest political level, and it was utilised as a defence at the SS-Einsatzgruppen Trial in terms of it being a lawful instruction issued in the extraordinary circumstances of war (Earl 2009, 197–210). The so-called *Führerbefehl* was not relied on in the subsequent court case brought against 22 of the leaders of the SS-Einsatzgruppen. The SS-Einsatzgruppen Trial was a trial of the senior leadership of the SS-Einsatzgruppen who were in custody at the end of the war. It was not intended to be more comprehensive than that, and the vast bulk of those who served in its ranks, and who took part in the atrocities it undertook as part of Operation Barbarossa and other murderous campaigns, were never charged with any offences whatsoever. The prosecution reasoned that if the order existed it simply confirmed the existence, and intent, of the genocidal programme undertaken by the SS-Einsatzgruppen at a higher level, and if it did not exist then that simply meant that the defendants in the case could not claim that they were following orders. Whether the *Führerbefehl* existed, or not, did little to placate the guilt of those involved in the mass-murders undertaken by the SS-Einsatzgruppen. It is inconceivable that the programme of mass-murder, and the costly logistic operation that supported it, did not have political support (Earl 2009, 55–56; 146–147; 201–215). The defence of following superior orders was given short shrift by the International Military Tribunal although it had an established basis in German Law. After the International Military Tribunal had done its work, such cases as were brought against members of the SS-Einsatzgruppen in the German courts allowed that soldiers, in times of war, do not make wholly independent decisions. This meant that SS-Einsatzgruppen members were understood as killing Jews, partisans or whoever else, only because of higher orders directed against groups that the soldiers had not independently determined (Langerbein 2004, 12). The Tribunals convened in respect of the former Yugoslavia and Rwanda specifically ruled out any superior orders defence; indeed, it is forbidden in the Rome Statute. As was the case in the SS-Einsatzgruppen Trial the amended Rome Statute determined that: "Orders to commit genocide or crimes against humanity are manifestly unlawful" (Article 33, Rome Statute of the International Criminal Court). Similarly, any defence of conducting a pre-emptive war of self-defence is also excluded under Article 2, Section 4 of the United Nations Charter of 1945. However, wars of self-defence seem to have been back with us for some time now, with the so-called war on terror.

The details of the gruesome crimes of the SS-Einsatzgruppen we will not dwell on, instead we will examine the trial of senior SS-Einsatzgruppen officers after the Second World War since it illuminates many points of perennial importance relating to the portioning of responsibility for actions undertaken by an obviously delinquent organisation. In any case, the SS-Einsatzgruppen seem to fulfil all the criteria we explored in Chap. 4 in terms of it conceiving of its criminal enterprise being its organisational rationale. Moreover, the members of the SS-Einsatzgruppen also straight-forwardly follow Sanchez-Brigado's formulation in terms of collective intentional action (Sanchez-Brigado 2010, 85). It should be further noted that, in terms of individual responsibility, the SS-Einsatzgruppen Trial defined this in terms of crimes against humanity and the prosecution sought to establish that that entailed understanding humanity as possessing sovereignty and itself an actor in terms of international law. The prosecution argued that there was a plethora of international agreements, declarations and treaties already established before the commencement of the Second World War that had already established standards of behaviour in war and the treatment of civilians and infants by both international convention and established norms of conduct. The prosecution held that the International Military Tribunal was simply making many of these norms and conventions explicit and was addressing the failure of the SS-Einsatzgruppen, and other parties involved in the mass-murders, to abide by normal standards of conduct and the principles established by international law that enshrines the protection of persons in terms of their human rights. The International Military Tribunal rejected the idea it was doing anything novel, indeed the judges stated that "… humanity is the sovereignty which has been offended this is not a new concept in the realm of morals, but it is an innovation in the empire of law" (Geras 2015). Therefore, it followed that if the International Military Tribunal was going to treat humanity as sovereign that this entailed going beyond the limitations of the nation state and that the protection it sought to afford must reside in international law. The International Military Tribunal vigorously argued for individual responsibility to be a prominent feature of the then, newly emerging, international legal framework. Moreover, it understood international law as a way of operationalising humanity's sovereign will to justice. All the defendants in the SS-Einsatzgruppen Trial were prosecuted as individuals responsible for their actions under international law and incapable of shielding themselves under a defence of following superior orders in a time of war. The mass-murders of the SS-Einsatzgruppen were a violation of sovereign human rights of innocents, pure and simple. As the Holocaust witnessed the systematic annihilation and dehumanisation of whole populations, and of the mentally ill and physically disabled, the International Military Tribunal understood its task as upholding a sense of *universal* humanity, as detailed in the Charter of the United Nations and articulated in international law, over and against the dehumanising doctrine of the Nazis which separated persons and afforded them differential levels of respect. The International Military Tribunal, in this way, became an important political aspect of a post-war recognition that persons are connected through their humanity. In this way, the SS-Einsatzgruppen Trial and the other Nuremberg trials feed into our contemporary International Criminal Court. The prosecutors sought to stress the conscience of the rest of humanity to the atrocities of the Holocaust. It emphasised the need to defend the universal bond of humanity, and the importance of the least of us, against those who wished to divide humanity.

In the case brought against the 22 leaders of the SS-Einstatzgruppen there was a necessity not only to link these men to the wicked policy of the Nazi regime but also, directly, to the genocidal actions of their subordinates. The prosecution reasoned that the mass-murder of Jews, partisans and other so-called enemies of the Reich stemmed *directly* from policies issued through the SS in all its various guises (RSHA, SD, Gestapo and so forth), and that all the members of the SS-Einstatzgruppen were freely acting subjects. The International Military Tribunal therefore declared the SS, in all its various guises, to be a criminal organisation and that the senior officers of the SS, who were on trial, were aware of the policy of mass-murder. The case against the 22 senior SS-Einsatzgruppen leaders was all about linking them to the actual units that undertook the killings; a case made easier by the meticulous record keeping of the SS-Einsatzgruppen which gave precise details of where and when mass-murders occurred. The prosecution, moreover, sought to establish that the SS-Einsatzgruppen were aware of the genocidal policy even before the war by linking the defendants to the murder of the mentally ill and physically handicapped before the advent of the Second World War (Taylor 1992, 75). It is important to note here the prosecution's ability to prove that the defendants were freely acting subjects. This voluntarism was key to proving that the 22 senior SS-Einsatzgruppen leaders followed the policies issued through the SS in all its various guises and therefore, and to this extent, agreed with them. Telford Taylor, the chief counsel to the International Military Tribunal, maintained that full awareness of the atrocities undertaken by the SS-Einsatzgruppen was important to their full responsibility and he noted that as the 22 defendants were so senior there was no question of this matter (Taylor 1992). Indeed, Himmler had noted in a variety of speeches and documentation that he intended that the SS would take overall responsibility for the Holocaust (Longerich 2012, 437–468). Therefore, being a senior SS-Einsatzgruppen leader was coterminous with undertaking crimes against humanity. The SS-Einsatzgruppen's own records demonstrated the numbers of persons murdered in considerable detail, including by age, by race, by religion and by gender. The SS-Einsatzgruppen's own records showed where each unit worked, in terms of the territory where mass-murders were committed, and the length of time units were deployed. Such meticulous record keeping meant that it was not possible for defendants to reasonably claim to be ignorant of these atrocities, nor to deny the doctrine promulgated through the policies issued to the SS-Einsatzgruppen by the Reich Main Security Office in Berlin (Earl 2009, 3–4).

The SS-Einsatzgruppen Trial was important legally for its twin-track approach of, on the one hand, prosecuting the responsible organisational person and, on the other hand, the individual prosecution of individuals. This approach had to sustain the fact that the SS-Einstatzgruppen constituted a criminally responsible corporate person independent of the members of it and that it was important to hold responsible those individuals who were part of the criminal organisation, SS-Einstatzgruppen. Although, the individual members were certainly carrying out actions that were specified by the Reich Main Security Office, and ultimately of the Nazi state, they were nonetheless personally responsible for their own actions (Tenenbaum 1955). It was also important that the 22 defendants were connected by common purpose, and by association, with the killing itself; since there is no evidence that any of them had personally killed in terms of pulling a trigger (Earl 2009, 145). The International Military Tribunal members were aided in their task, since all the 22 defendants were committed Nazis, party members of long-standing who were steeped in the ideology of Nazism and the genocidal goals of the SS. The ideology of racial superiority was linked to the mass-murders: it was the reason for it. This ideological commitment, on the part of the 22 defendants, was evidence that the mass murders undertaken by the SS-Einstatzgruppen were not simply the *ad hoc* atrocities that can sometime happen in war but part of a well-worked-out plan. The mass murders were deliberate, organised and the outcome of ideological reasoning (Longerich 2012, 515–540). The prosecution showed how, given this forethought, the Nazi regime was a threat to all humanity in its dehumanising determination about the worth of persons simply based on their connection, or alleged connection, to this or that group, and the resultant mass-murder that such a rationale entailed. It was part of the prosecution's case that *humanity* is necessarily about the connection of persons in a world of interconnected lives that are inseparable and equally valued irrespective of race, religion or other cultural or anthropological variable. The International Military Tribunal was, at heart, a defence of human rights in their most basic form (Geras 2015).

The 22 senior members of the SS-Einsatzgruppen had freely followed the Nazi doctrine of racial superiority and in so doing they freely chose to murder innocent people who they considered both racially inferior and, because of that, wedded to Bolshevistic politics. The International Military Tribunal prosecution was focused on the condemnation of the intractable efforts, in furtherance of systematic mass-murder, by the SS and the embers of the SS-Einsatzgruppen. Although racial murder had been seen before in human history the ideological commitment to the annihilation of so many persons in such a mechanised and logistically coherent fashion was new. This ideological commitment to annihilation ran right through the SS and all those who were part of it were party to it. As Persico noted, Hans Frank spoke of the "seduction" of this ideology aimed at the German people (Persico 2000, 185). All the murders were freely undertaken by the SS-Einsatzgruppen and Earl notes wide public support for it and, after all, "anti-Semitism was a fundamental tenet of Nazism" (Earl 2009, 137). Daniel Goldhagen notes a fusion of ideological commitment and an ethic of obedience (Goldhagen 1996). The SS-Einsatzgruppen Trial has received a great deal of legal and historical attention and there seems to be common agreement that, following the defeat of Germany in 1918, both extreme nationalism and a virulent form of anti-Semitism took hold in Germany. There was widespread resentment at the harsh reparations that the Versailles Treaty imposed on Germany and the rumour spread that the Jews were responsible for all of it (Kershaw 2008). The invasion of the Soviet Union was a war of annihilation, a war of revenge. Bolshevism was equated with the Jews (Longerich 2012, 625–632). What is undoubtedly the case is that these elements of historically structured anti-Semitism came into play and, in effect, the SS-Einsatzgruppen undertook mass-murder but it was nonetheless patterned by an ideology of rightful violence that suffused the structure of the SS, indeed the structure of the Nazi state. The prosecutors were keen to maintain a distinction between war crimes and crimes against humanity; the former being a common feature of many wars whereas the latter was a fundamental assault on humanity as a whole, which is different in kind and is best understood in terms of an assault on the rights of all persons (Earl 2009, 217–264). This is clearly shown in the extensive planning and organisation of the mass-murders, which departed from all international norms of law. The SS-Einsatzgruppen were undertaking a racial war completely at odds with any reasonable understanding of conduct in war: theirs was a war against pre-identified groups of so-called racial inferiors. The defendants were not merely guilty of breaching legal norms, they had breached a law of humanity through their dehumanising actions. The defendants were *all* party to a criminal joint enterprise and held that more preciously than their understanding of the rights of other members of humankind.

After the SS-Einsatzgruppen Trial

The verdict in the SS-Einsatzgruppen Trial was that all the defendants were found guilty as charged and 13 of the 22 were initially given death sentences. However, following various interventions by German bishops, by the US led Simpson Commission and by the Judge Advocate's Office a clemency panel reduced many of the original sentences and of the original 22 defendants only 4 were executed (Otto Ohlendorf, Erich Naumann, Werner Braune and Paul Blobel). Heinz Jost, for example, who was an SS general was released in January 1952 and then became a successful estate agent in Dusseldorf (Earl 2009, 274–293). Likewise, Heinz Schubert who had personally been involved in the murder of over 90,000 people in southern Ukraine (Earl 2009, 258–264). Of the 3000 men who served with the SS-Einsatzgruppen only 200 were ever charged with war-time atrocities. They slipped back into civilian life taking up jobs in the police, local government and the military. After the Second World War, there was concern about the threat that the Soviet Union represented to Europe, especially with the territorial ground it had managed to achieve with Poland, Hungary, much of Eastern Europe and a divided Germany. The former Allied Powers considered this the bigger threat, rather than chasing down former Nazi war criminals. Appalled by these commutations of sentence, the Chief Prosecutor in the SS-Einsatzgruppen Trial, Benjamin Ferencz, wrote to Telford Taylor, the Chief Counsel in the case, in December 1951 stating that: "You may recall that the deadline for *cleansing* up Simferopol was Christmas 1941 and that Schubert managed to kill all the Jews by then. So, for Christmas ten years later he goes Scot free. Who says there is no Santa Claus" (Bloxham 2004, 163).

What the SS-Einsatzgruppen Trial, and the other Nuremberg Trials, did establish was an agreed set of legal principles which would thereafter be the basis for both local and international legal statute. The set of Nuremberg trials became the accepted model for other national and international courts dealing with the war crimes of rogue governments, a point Landsman makes (Landsman 2005, 242–245). Although, it must also be conceded, post-war Germany tended to achieve very low conviction rates, given the numbers involved, and to follow up with light sentences when they did convict (Landsman 242). Nonetheless, the International Military Tribunal formed the backdrop to the drafting of the 1948 Genocide Convention, and indeed for the 1948 United Nations Universal Declaration of Human Rights. The world had been outraged by the atrocities undertaken by the Nazis, and by the military government in Japan (Amatrudo and Blake 2015, 18–19). The 1948 Genocide Convention followed the International Military Tribunal in separating genocide from war crimes, in other words distinguishing human rights in the form of crimes against humanity from aggressive, illegal, war-making (Geras 2015). However, with the passage of time the atrocities of the SS-Einsatzgruppen, and other war criminals, faded from memory and the post-war period soon became entangled in the Cold War and its call to combat the Soviet Union and China. It has also been argued that after the gruelling struggle of the Second World War and the film, that soon became available with the defeat of the Nazis, of the concentration camps there was a feeling that, hard as it might be, people had to move on and not look back. There was still rationing in Europe for many years after the end of the Second World War and the population were more taken with remaking their own lives and communities than reflecting upon the highest ideals of human dignity (Kershaw 2015). It was only at the nadir of the Cold War, when the Berlin Wall had already fallen, that the excesses of ethnic cleansing and organised mass-rape in Bosnia and Herzegovina, which were the issues that the International Military Tribunal had dealt with, became, once again, a reality in Europe. As a result of the ethnic cleansing and organised mass-rape in Bosnia and Herzegovina the United Nations Security Council fashioned the International Criminal Tribunal for the former Yugoslavia which charged many of those involved with genocide and crimes against humanity, in a way akin to the SS-Einsatzgruppen Trial. A little later, the United Nations set up the International Criminal Tribunal for Rwanda in late 1994 following the mass-murder of up to 90,000 Tutsis by Hutus and where both the form of the legal statute and the formal procedures mirrored those of the International Military Tribunal (Landsman, 247–248).

The most important point is that the distinction between genocide and crimes against humanity are thought of as different, in kind, from the crimes of aggressive, illegal war-making by the Tribunals convened in respect of the former Yugoslavia and Rwanda. Therefore, the SS-Einsatzgruppen Trial and the other trials undertaken in the Nuremberg process are so important: they are foundational, a precedent for all other trials where crimes against humanity are at issue. It is noteworthy that the Rome Statute for the International Court, which came into effect in 2002, almost 60 years after the end of the Second World War, understood the four core international crimes of genocide, crimes against humanity, war crimes and crimes of aggression. In so doing, it took its inspiration from the original International Military Tribunal following the Second World War (Schabas 2004). The International Criminal Court, however, soon encountered disapproval from the United States and, to a lesser extent, Russia, China and other countries, that understand this as, somehow, infringing their own sovereignty and right to determine the nature of any *contested* events, including crimes against humanity (Bosco 2014).

The real legacy of the SS-Einsatzgruppen Trial must be in its opening up of the files and making public the crimes of the Nazi state under the rule of law and showing how ordinary men, not devils, undertook atrocities. It exposed the barbarous nature of the racist ideology perpetrated by the Hitler regime. The SS-Einsatzgruppen Trial was undertaken before Lemkin's famous article, that gave the world the word *genocide*, had been fully accepted by politicians and jurists (Lemkin 1946, 227–270). Genocide, at the time of the SS-Einsatzgruppen Trial, was yet to be defined and to some extent there was no legal vocabulary for the atrocities the Nazis committed. It was new to human history. Therefore, the SS-Einsatzgruppen Trial was a fairly traditional trial in many ways so that it can be argued that it failed to grasp the logistic, moral and political ramifications of murder on such a scale. Mass-murders undertaken, moreover, on the basis of a supposed Ayran racial superiority in a so-called defensive war against the alleged evils of Bolshevism and the Jews. This was a form of madness to many who tried to understand it without the benefit of the historical, legal and political understanding we have today. (Kershaw 2015). Yet the judges in the case sought, in the face of all that, to meet out justice, not revenge. The court heard pleas and it reduced sentences, including the commuting of the death sentence in several cases, and it was criticised for that (Buscher 1989, 3–4). In truth, with Europe in tatters after mass aerial bombing and a horrific war where there were millions of displaced people and realistic fears of another war breaking out between the West and the Soviet Union, it is tribute to the United States and the Allies that they went to the trouble of bringing cases to trial. In the Soviet Union, and across the now Communist Eastern European regimes, there were many thousands of extrajudicial executions (Pogany 1997). The early release of many of the men found guilty by the International Military Tribunal is not something we can blame on the court, rather it was a lack of political courage. The political resolve that was abundant in 1945 was waning by the 1950s and, in any case, the West German state wanted to move on and forget the horrors of past times; after all this was the time of the *Wirtschaftswunder*, the German "economic miracle" and the newly minted Deutsche Mark (Kershaw 2015). However, the SS-Einsatzgruppen Trial was only one aspect of the transformation of jurisprudence and political understanding that arose in the middle of the twentieth century and later there were trials of minor members of the Waffen-SS, Gestapo, Ordnungspolizei and SS-Einstatzgruppen in Germany, by Germans, on behalf of the German Federal Republic in Bonn. This transformation of jurisprudence and political understanding that came about following the end of the Second World War, and which the SS-Einsatzgruppen Trial was only a small part of, resulted, ultimately, in the ICC in The Hague. The SS-Einsatzgruppen Trial was not without serious flaws but, in the circumstances then pertaining, it did well enough. Nonetheless, it prosecuted the *delinquent* organisation that was the SS-Einsatzgruppen and the individuals who were party to its work, and who were all too aware of its *purpose*. In doing this in terms of corporate and personal responsibility the International Military Tribunal did a great service to the many trials that have had to deal with crimes against humanity, like those in the former Yugoslavia, Rwanda and others.

Membership of Illegal, or Criminal, Organisations (Terrorist Groups)

One way of distinguishing a corporation from a group is in terms of a corporation being thought of as a person with moral agency whereas a group is merely a collection of people. This assumes that the corporation has a social aspect to its composition rather than it being an aggregation. Locke defined persons as having an ability to think and reflect consistently through time and place (Locke 1975, 2). Locke understood that if this criterion can be satisfied then a corporation counts as a person. This has long been a popular test of personhood, most recently employed by the philosopher, Peter French (French 1979, 207–215). It is important that the Lockean tradition does not equate personhood, and the things that flow from it such as responsibility, with flesh and blood and there is a clear sense that corporations can have agency in, and of, themselves (French 1992). Corporations, and this includes companies, French explains, are "moral persons" because they are held to account and routinely commended and censured for the actions that they undertake (French 1984, 32). French's main point being that unless we hold corporations as "moral persons" we will have no redress when they do wrong and that law recognises this in affording the corporation certain enforceable rights. French holds that corporations are not simply aggregations of persons but, as we saw in Chap. 4, have internal decision-making structures (in French, corporate internal decision making) and, moreover, individuated roles within the corporation (French 1979, 211; 1984, 13). To be a moral person the corporation may act, by itself, and in so doing it structures the matrix of goals, values and intentions that individual persons operate by. It is worth quoting French here:

"(1) an organisational system that delineates stations and levels of decision making; and (2) a set of decision/action recognitions rules of two types, procedural and policy. These recognition rules provide the tests that a decision or an action was made for the corporate reasons within the corporate decision structure. The policy recognitors are particularly relevant to the attribution of corporate intentionality .... The organisational structure of a corporation gives the grammar of its decision making, and the recognition of rules provide its logic. The CID (corporate internal decision making) structure provides a subordination and synthesis of the decisions and acts of various human beings and other intentional systems into a corporate action, an event that under one of its aspects may be truthfully described as having been done for corporate reasons or to bring about corporate ends, expectations, purposes and so on" (French 1992, 213).

French neatly demonstrates by this reasoning how the actions of persons, individual persons, when undertaken as members of a corporation are therefore fashioned by the corporation; and accordingly, we attribute agency to the corporation. We may, however, reason that it is not necessary for a corporation to be understood as a person, as French argues, for it to have moral agency if we hold that it nonetheless possesses mindedness (Goldie 2000). We can simply note that a corporation acts with definite goals in mind and that we can establish that it is enmeshed in a matrix of duties, rights and obligations. These goals, duties, rights and obligations structure the corporation. Although, like Goldie, one may note that true moral experience requires a range of affective characteristics that cannot be shown in a corporation, such as remorse, and which have an emotional content. Moreover, that it is precisely these emotional characteristics that are essential to personhood; especially since we think of the moral person as altering his actions and adjusting his goals in the light of them, being a responsive moral actor. Need this matter for the criminal law? It need not, for as Sheehy notes: "Strip the corporation of its putative personhood, and we shall be left with its mind and the character of that mind" (Sheehy 2006, 149). This was also explored by Brown in relation to actor-network theory, concerning human and technological hybrids, in an area of criminological theory she pioneered, hybrid networks analysis (2006, 223–244). Brown was ahead of the field at the time and now such issues are of crucial importance as crime moves online. Squires gives us reason to doubt that this model is always useful in terms of the prosecution of looser associations, like street gangs, in terms of their criminal actions simply because it is too glib to assume structure and goal setting, and how, this has led to inadequate justice (Squires 2016, 937–956).

In criminal law, organisations of various types, such as terrorist groups, organised criminal groups and delinquent organisations, are held as culpable; though there is recognition that they come in a variety of types, such as cartels, formal networks, loose associations. These organisations, which share features with law-abiding organisations, are the basis for joint criminal enterprise prosecutions. We note their form in terms of how it is patterned by goals, duties, rights and obligations. We duly understand how an organisation can be considered a "threat to society" (Levi 2002, 878–879, 912–913). Harding raises two considerable problems we need to consider. In terms of the delinquent corporation he notes that: "Their delinquent character means that they are naturally shady and furtive actors in the material world, so that any 'outside' understanding of their form and operation is achieved with greater difficulty than is the case with companies and State institutions." He goes on to further note how for criminal groups:

"There is a greater element of speculation and surmise in relation to criminal groups, whether in the context of public perception, official policy or even academic research. In that sense, the subject matter has a slipperiness which should sound a note of caution … the delinquent character of this kind of organisation may raise ethical objection to the argument that they be treated alongside 'legitimate' companies or public bodies of governance, in that such a process in some way may approve or even serve to legitimise the existence of activities which are from most points of view objection-able" (Harding 2007, 193).

The examples Harding suggests are criminal organisations and terrorist groups which, he contends, are given: "… some form of legal personality may encounter the objection that legal orders are thereby accommodating the existence of entities which should simply be the subject of legal control and repression" (Harding 2007, 193). Harding misses the sociological usefulness of this form of analysis and, moreover, is overlooking the existential reality of delinquent groups, which is independent of their moral worth. There seems nothing controversial in noting the reality of a social group, on the one hand, and bemoaning its failure to act morally, in other words its moral status, on the other (Warren 1997). James Q. Wilson long ago advocated this position in his *Political Organisations* of 1973.

Terrorism

If we explore this issue in relation to terrorism, rather than organised crime *per se*, we can note the operation of the delinquent organisation as a body with criminal agency and legal personality. We can define terrorism sufficiently to undertake this task, although this is disputed by some academics (Hodgson and Tadros 2013). Although terrorist groups are not ordered legally, which means they are more difficult to identify, they nonetheless exhibit legal personality and have structures akin to legitimate organisations: indeed, this has been the regular practice of the United Nations for the past couple of decades, stemming from the Security Council's Resolution 1267 of 1999. In the same timeframe (i.e. in the past couple of decades or so), we have witnessed terrorist groups taking on *pseudo*-politico-territorial roles in a number of countries, such as Somalia and, more recently, Libya (Hmoud 2013)

It is important to say something more about the nature of terrorist groups, since they take many forms. The most straightforward way of doing this is by thinking about exclusive and inclusive definitions, in the academic literature. This simple delineation is very useful for our purposes. There are innumerable ways one might set about defining a terrorist group but whatever measure is used it is likely that three factors would be key. These are (1) the use of intentional violence, (2) a desire to spread *terror* in the general population for broader political reasons and (3) a strong political motivation behind (1) and (2), though what counts as political is somewhat disputed and we may venture some terrorism could be defined by its religious content, for example (Schmid and Jongman 1988). In Wilson's terms, terrorist groups are certainly definable and formal, in the sense that they organise and structure their members' actions (Wilson 1973, 31). The precise form of the group may alter but sufficient to say that is of less importance than its organising and structuring properties, for which it bears responsibility. There are only rare cases of completely isolated persons undertaking terrorist actions and even in those cases it can be argued that there is an attenuated organising and structuring through a broader ideological grouping or community. Terrorism encompasses a huge range of activity and is more difficult to study as it is found in all societies, across time and geography. Trying to account for terrorism is, then, a hapless task. Its methods and tactics differ markedly from group to group, urban and rural guerrillas. It is fair to say that few academics and policy makers care to venture a definition of terrorism beyond some version of the base model that I have set out. Terrorism will always be a contested term, always open to the revisions of history and experience. Nelson Mandela and Menachem Begin, among others, are noted as terrorists. Another very important reason why terrorism is often left undefined is that few, if any, groups are essentially terroristic. Rather it is the case that terrorism is used often as a tactic to advance ideas that are frustrated by the dominant political power. A good example might be the Irish Republican Army (IRA) which operated, at various times, as a nationalist group against what it saw as English colonialists. A sympathetic and historically nuanced case is made in these terms by the journalist and historian Tim Pat Coogan in his majestic *The I.R.A.* Coogan places the IRA within the historical context of the broader Irish nationalist movement for independence from the United Kingdom, in the twentieth century. The terrorist actions the IRA undertook he subordinates, in the final instance, to notions of political self-determination. Irish terrorism, as detailed by Coogan, was not an end in itself (Coogan

2000). One of the reasons that terrorism is left undefined is that this denotes an understanding that there is no such thing as an exclusively terrorist group. Moreover, as Coogan noted in relation to the IRA, academics have often noted how terrorism is but an aspect of a broader political struggle. The academic literature on terrorism falls, fairly neatly, into two sets of literature: one using an inclusive definition and the other an exclusive definition. An inclusive definition being one that counts any group that utilises terrorism as a terrorist group whereas an exclusive definition is one that employs a variety of distinctions, such as groups employing exclusively terrorist tactics, in contra-distinction to groups who employ other sorts of violence or non-violent activity, such as sabotaging railway lines or electricity supply and so forth. In examining inclusive definitions of terrorism, we note a willingness to broadly attribute terrorism to a group, though often with technical provisos, such as thinking of terrorism as either actor or action derived or domestic or religiously inspired, or some such (de la Calle and Sanchez-Cuenca 2011). The important thing is not the type of terrorism employed, or the form of the group, but the use of terrorism in, and of, itself is important to those who hold to an inclusive definition. One common inclusive formula is to say something along the lines of a terrorist group is one that uses terrorist tactics and to loosely define "terrorist tactics" as meaning the deliberate targeting of civilians in furtherance of a political objective (Carter 2012, 130). Other academics have invoked a measure of psychological distress "in an audience that extends beyond the target victims" (Price 2012, 9). Weinberg gives one of the most commonly cited inclusive definitions: "Terrorist groups are organizations that rely, partially or exclusively on terrorism to achieve their political ends" (Weinberg 1991, 437). Weinberg's definition has been influential because it neatly sets out how a terrorist group may employ terror tactics "partially or exclusively" in furtherance of "political ends." This might appear unremarkable but, for our purposes, it is useful as it refers not to individuals but to the group in question, and the group, not simply the action, must have a specific *political end*. This is very helpful in delineating terrorist groups from criminal ones, although here too argument rages (Longmire and Longmire 2008, 35–51). This matter of delineating terrorism from criminality, *per se*, is an important one and academics employing an inclusive definition wish to reject criminal groups in their definition. The other point that we detect in inclusive definitions is that they tend to conceive of terrorist groups as a sub-national phenomenon and thereby exclude state terror from their sphere of study. They understand terrorism as a matter of sub-national political groups that employ terror for specific *political* reasons. The inclusive definition holds to sub-national groups, with political ends that employ terror tactics. The inclusive definition is reasonably expansive but nonetheless it has a clear three-fold measure of what counts as terrorism. This is important in the context of policing since terrorism must be given an operational value by the public authorities and be able to exclude a variety of campaigning and political groups. Governments and transnational organisations often employ inclusive definitions since states have little option but to treat any group that engages in terrorism as a terrorist group, whether or not it holds territory or conducts other, non-terrorist, operations. It seems that an exclusive definition of terrorist groups is also *operationally* more satisfactory for academic work if we accept no definition is likely to be perfect in capturing all the elements of a terrorist group's rationale.

Let us turn to examining exclusive definitions of terrorist groups. The most widespread distinction employed is between those terrorist groups that possess territory and those that do not. There is also the distinction between groups that exclusively, or predominately, use terror tactics, and those who employ other sorts of tactics, whether or notthey employ violence. This is the main exclusive definition employed by academics between those who hold territory and those who do not; terrorist groups are associated with groups that do not (de la Calle and Sanchez-Cuenca 2011, 465). This definition holds that terrorism is dictated, in the sense of setting out the determining power conditions, by territorial holders (states) and that the sub-national groups, terrorist groups, resort to terror tactics because of that power relation. There are also those who argue that some groups typically referred to as terrorist groups are not, since they hold territory, for example the FARC or Sudan Revolutionary Front, which ought properly to be referred to as guerrilla groups. The point being to distinguish the clandestine terrorist group, from those groups who are not; to this extent it is an ontological distinction. It tends to the distinction between those groups that exclusively employ terror tactics and those who do not. This is important as it may well delineate those organisations that employ terror as a strategy to overcome a *perceived* form of regime power disproportionally impacting upon them, and therefore it cannot also encompass groups such as anti-colonial groups. In other words, since these groups do not hold territory they take up terror tactics: this follows from the disproportionality in power relations (Crenshaw 1991, 75). It is important to note here that it is typical that exclusive definitions may well employ inclusive conditions. Exclusive definitions often maintain the elements of an inclusive definition but place extra caveats upon it, so as to restrict the range of viable groups. An example of the divergence of opinion between academics might be in relation to Mexican criminal drug networks that may be termed "terrorist" because they employ terror tactics but might ordinarily be thought of as simply criminal (Longmire and Longmire 2008, 35–51). The issue is a tricky one given that many terrorist groups are also linked to criminal activity. The Provisional IRA, and a range of other Republican groups, became embroiled in criminal activity to finance their campaigns of terror (Horgan and Taylor 1999, 1–38).

In defining terrorist groups, we are doing important work, but to define such groups differentially (i.e. inclusively or exclusively) will lead us to different conclusions. It is also clear that if, for example, we think of terrorist groups as sub-national phenomenon then at what point of engagement with a state does this fail to capture the phenomenon? We might ask, where does one draw the line between criminal activity and political action? What we do note is that however we define terrorist groups, *qua* groups, they seem to have agency. Moreover, its members too have a form of agency structured by the group. We note how the organisation both constitutes and facilitates actions and attitudes (Sanchez-Brigado 2010, 85). Harding is right, in any case, to hold that terrorist groups: "(H)ave a sufficiently durable and consistent form, clarity of purpose and solid internal constitution as to merit serious consideration as moral and legal agents, and hence responsibility, distinct from their individual membership" (Harding 2007, 203). However, the way terrorist groups are defined in terms of whether they hold territory, or not, or whether, or not, they *exclusively* use terror tactics is not discussed by

Harding and he, rather unfortunately, spends a great deal of time exploring al Queda, Hizbullah and the Taliban all of whom are, to some extent, defined regionally and in terms of a religious commitment (Harding 2007, 204–205). At various times, the groups Harding mentions include the state and that changes a lot. Nonetheless, Harding holds that terrorist groups can indeed be afforded a legal definition and that there can be a useful distribution of legal responsibility between collective entities, in other words a given terrorist group, and its individual members (Harding 2007).

Common Threads

We saw in Chap. 4 that the two core issues relating to thinking about the criminal responsibility of organisations are (1) a stable underlying structure and (2) some sense of internal decision making. In both cases we have looked at, the state sponsored SS-Einsatzgruppen and non-state terrorist groups, it is the organisation that *facilitates* action. It is improbable that individuals on their own would undertake these criminal actions. In both cases, the sociological determination of action is best thought of in terms of the group, the delinquent organisation. The resolution to the allocation of responsibility problem between individuals and groups, organisations, is best addressed in terms of joint criminal enterprise. As Harding notes: "The underlying justification for joint enterprise liability and its analogous forms is thus a matter of individual personal responsibility but in respect of an act of complicity, and it is this complicity in the enterprise which provides the basis for both liability and the evidence" (Harding 2007, 265). One issue we are left with is that, as we saw in relation to terrorist groups, there is a great deal of dispute about the legal standing of many groups and currently we have a disputed international legal settlement as to the overall legal framework that ought to be employed. As we saw in relation to the SS-Einsatzgruppen, a great deal of the response is determined by the necessities of events at the time and of the immediate context at hand. In the case of the SS-Einsatzgruppen we noted how the political and sociological settlement in a divided post-war Europe meant that justice was not seriously pursued. What we have shown is that determining the responsibility of organisations, and groups, inevitably means thinking about the issues that are broader than the legal breach at hand and instead begin to think more sociologically and philosophically, in terms of agency, and not simply in terms of law, *per se*. This is the surest way forward.

Bibliography

Amatrudo, A., & Blake, L. (2015). *Human Rights and the Criminal Justice System*. London: Routledge.

Bloxham, D. (2004). *Genocide on Trial*. Oxford: OUP.

Bosco, D. (2014). *Rough Justice; The International Criminal Court's Battle to Fix the World, One Prosecution at a Time*. Oxford: OUP.

Brown, S. (2006). The Criminology of Hybrids: Rethinking Crime and Law in Techno-social Networks. *Theoretical Criminology, 10*(2), 223–244.

Buscher, F. (1989). *The United States War Crimes Trial Program in Germany, 1946–1955*. New York: Greenwood Press.

de la Calle, L., & Sanchez-Cuenca, I. (2011). What We Talk About When We Talk About Terrorism. *Politics and Society, 39*(3), 451–472.

Carter, D. (2012). A Blessing or a Curse? State Support for Terrorist Groups. *International Organization, 66*(1), 129–151.

Coogan, T. P. (2000). *The I.R.A.* London: Harper Collins.

Crenshaw, M. (1991). How Terror Declines. *Terrorism and Political Violence, 3*(1), 69–87.

Earl, H. (2009). *The Nuremberg SS-Einsatzgruppen Trial, 1945–1958: Atrocity Law and History*. New York: Cambridge University Press.

French, P. (1979). The Corporation as a Moral Person. *American Philosophical Quarterly, 16*(3), 207–215.

French, P. (1984). *Collective and Corporate Personality*. New York: Columbia University Press.

French, P. (1992). *Responsibility Matters*. Lawrence: University Press of Kansas.

Geras, N. (2015). *Crimes Against Humanity: Birth of a Concept*. Manchester: Manchester University Press.

Goldhagen, D. (1996). *Hitler's Willing Executioners: Ordinary Germans and the Holocaust*. New York: Alfred Knopf.

Goldie, P. (2000). *The Emotions: A Philosophical Exploration*. Oxford: Clarendon Press.

Harding, C. (2007). *Criminal Enterprise: Individuals, Organisations and Criminal Responsibility*. Cullompton: Willan Press.

Hmoud, M. (2013). Are New Principles Really Needed? The Potential of the Established Distinction Between Responsibility for Attacks by Nonstate Actors and the Law of Self-Defence. *American Journal of International Law, 107*(3), 576–579.

Hodgson, S., & Tadros, V. (2013). The Impossibility of Defining Terrorism. *New Criminal Law Review, 16*(3), 494–526.

Horgan, J., & Taylor, M. (1999). Playing the 'Green Card' – Financing the Provisional IRA. *Terrorism and Political Violence, 11*(2), 1–38.

Kershaw, I. (2008). *Hitler, The Germans and the Final Solution*. New Haven: Yale University Press.

Kershaw, I. (2015). *To Hell and Back: Europe 1914– 1949*. London: Allen Lane.

Landsman, S. (2005). *Crimes of the Holocaust: The Law Confronts Hard Cases*. Philadelphia: University of Pennsylvania Press.

Langerbein, H. (2004). *Hitler's Death Squads: The Logic of Mass Murder*. College Station: Texas A&M University Press.

Lemkin, R. (1946). Genocide. *American Scholar, 2*(15), 227–270.

Levi, M. (2002). The Organization of Serious Crime. In M. Maguire, R. Morgan, & R. Reiner (Eds.), *The Oxford Handbook of Criminology* (3rd ed., pp. 878–913). Oxford: OUP.

Locke, J. (1975). *An Essay Concerning Human Understanding*. Oxford: OUP.

Longerich, P. (2012). *Heinrich Himmler*. Oxford: OUP.

Longmire, S., & Longmire, J. (2008). Redefining Terrorism: Why Mexican Drug Trafficking Is More Than Just Organized Crime. *Journal of Strategic Security, 1*(1), 35–51.

Marrus, M. (2000). *The Holocaust in History*. Toronto: Key Porter Press.

Persico, J. (2000). *Nuremberg: Infamy on Trial*. London: Penguin Books.

Pogany, I. (1997). *Righting Wrongs in Eastern Europe*. Manchester: Manchester University Press.

Price, B. (2012). Targeting Top Terrorists: How Leadership Decapitation Contributes to Counterterrorism. *International Security, 36*(4), 9–46.

Rossino, A. (2003). *Hitler Strikes Poland: Blitzkrieg, Ideology and Atrocity*. Lawrence: University of Kansas Press.

Rutherford, J. (2014). *Combat and Genocide on the Eastern Front*. Cambridge: Cambridge University Press.

Sanchez-Brigado, R. E. (2010). *Groups, Rules and Legal Practice*. London: Springer.

Schabas, W. (2004). *An Introduction to the International Criminal Court*. Cambridge: Cambridge University Press.

Schmid, A., & Jongman, A. (1988). *Political Terrorism: A Guide to Actors, Authors, Concepts, Databases, Theories and Literature*. New Brunswick: Transaction Press.

Sheehy, P. (2006). *The Reality of Social Groups*. Chippenham: Ashgate.

Squires, P. (2016). *Voodoo Liability*: Joint Enterprise Prosecution as an Aspect of Intensified Criminalisation. *The Politics and Jurisprudence of Group Offending: Onati Socio-Legal Series, 6*(4), 937–956.

Taylor, T. (1992). *The Anatomy of the Nuremberg Trials: A Personal Memoir*. Toronto: Little, Brown & Co.

Tenenbaum, J. (1955). The Einsatzgruppen. *Jewish Social Studies, 17*(1), 43–64.

Warren, M. (1997). *Moral Status*. Oxford: Clarendon Press.

Weinberg, L. (1991). Turning to Terror: The Conditions Under Which Political Parties Turn to Terrorist Activities. *Comparative Politics, 23*(4), 423–438.

Wilson, J. Q. (1973). *Political Organizations*. New York: Basic Books.

6

The Gang in Criminological Literature

Of all the topics that contemporary Criminology deals with, arguably, the gang is the most researched. Moreover, gangs are considered in a variety of places, such as policing studies, youth work and migration: they are inescapable, being blamed, at various times, for all manner of things from murder and rape to drug dealing and people trafficking. Others still see gangs as a form of *resistance*, a social movement and helpful ad hoc socialiser of young people (Brotherton 2007). The extent of gangs is perennially disputed in the literature. There are those who see gangs everywhere and others who see the phenomenon as far more restricted. It both rests on whether scholars use a fat or a thin version of the gang in their work (Hallsworth and Young 2008). The phenomenon of gangs itself is hardly helped by there being no agreed working typology. Moreover, as I noted previously "… the *polluting* influence of funding from the police and a range of government agencies has meant that criminologists have had little incentive to be unduly critical of the basic ontological settlement around gangs" (Amatrudo 2015a, b, 105). There is also the phenomenon of the fetishisation and sexualisation of young, virile male bodies, often black, by, usually, white, middle-class observers, inside and outside of the academy. Many academics and policy makers are all

© The Author(s) 2018
A. Amatrudo, *Criminal Actions and Social Situations*,
https://doi.org/10.1057/978-1-137-45731-8_6

too willing to sensationalise the lives of young people and fit them neatly into a category; the gang as an object to stare at, to study and assess (Panfil 2014; Mayeda et al. 2001). Many scholars are all too willing to go along with the script. This issue of seeing gangs everywhere is a huge concern. At a time of falling crime rates the gang seems to be given greater and greater attention. The issue of joint criminal enterprise is intertwined with the issue of gangs, leading Squires to write of "voodoo criminal liability" concerning the over-criminalisation of young black men in our urban centres with their accompanying over-prosecution and over-incarceration rates (Squires 2016). We must never forget that Stan Cohen's *Folk Devils and Moral Panics* was about gangs, mods and rockers. Cohen's view was that the media's focus upon mods and rockers made them seem a far bigger problem than they were. So, it has been with a succession of groups over the years since Cohen's book appeared. It is worth citing, in full, Cohen's analysis in a passage from the start of the book, which is seminal:

> "Societies appear to be subject, every now and then, to periods of moral panic. A condition episode, person or group of persons emerges to become defined as a threat to societal values and interests; its nature is presented in a stylized and stereotypical fashion by the mass media; the moral barricades are manned by editors, bishops, politicians and other right-thinking people; socially accredited experts pronounce their diagnoses and solutions; ways of coping are evolved or (more often) resorted to; the condition then disappears, submerges or deteriorates and becomes more visible. Sometimes the object of the panic is quite novel and at other times it is something which has been in existence long enough, but suddenly appears in the limelight. Sometimes the panic passes over and is forgotten except in folklore and collective memory; at other times, it has more serious and long-lasting repercussions and might produce such changes as those in legal and social policy or even in the way the society conceives itself. One of the most recurrent types of moral panic in Britain since the war has been associated with the emergence of various forms of youth culture (originally almost exclusively working class, but often recently middle class or student based) whose behaviour is deviant or delinquent" (Cohen 1973, 9).

Crewe has argued in his *Becoming Criminal* that the study of gangs is allied to the project of social control, noting that:

"The processes of social control and conformity that are inherent in behaviour to the generalized other, I would suggest, are analogous to the formation of such nodes in dissipative systems, where significant numbers of people interact in concerted and complex ways ... the pressure to behave to the generalized other will produce nodes of similar aspirations, and similar behaviour; normalized behaviour. Refusal to conform and the production of new definitions of the situation through refusal to negotiate will provide new nodes around which conformity to a new generalized other can coalesce, producing what in the past has termed subcultures" (Crewe 2013, 184).

For Crewe, the engagement that the state has with gangs is ultimately about their reformation into non-gang members. There is general agreement that gangs, and their sub-cultures, are in large measure formed in relation to the unfair external power relations that relate to skewed economics and an unjust political settlement that excludes many citizens. Therefore, it makes sense to think of terms in a much broader social context. Reiner puts it well:

"The public face of crime ... is dominated by the crimes of afflicting the poor, who disproportionately pay the price through the pains of victimization and of punishment. How is this double whammy of social injustice legitimated, in particular, to the poorer and excluded sections of society? Certainly, a crucial part is played by the inculcation of ideological perspectives portraying the criminal law as universally beneficial protection against serious and frightening wrongs which are perpetrated by individuals who choose to do harm to others. The criminal process is legitimated by representing it as a fair application of the law to malefactors, operating in accordance with technical procedures that are impartial and effective" (Reiner 2016, 188).

Another point that could be made about Reiner's analysis is the differential attitudes that the public authorities exhibit towards different sorts of criminal activities, especially drug usage and drug dealing (Jacques and Wright 2015). The "gang" is regularly invoked as a defence of the disproportionate treatment of young people, especially young black men, in terms of stop and search (Bowling and Phillips 2007). Importantly, we note how the extent of gangs and their internal composition is of interest but, perhaps, less so than relationship of the treatment of the gang problem to broader economic and political issues and considerations of race. If we keep a focus upon Stan Cohen's *Folk Devils and Moral Panics* then we note that the gang is, when all is said and done, often a product of the media's outrage. There may well be issues around gang criminality but it is easy to see them as a focus for moral panic. Moreover, the appetite for information about the degenerate lives of the underclass is seemingly insatiable, as has been noted in terms of how the gang is related to a straight *audience* (Hallsworth 2013) and how urban life is patterned by stereotypes, as in the construction of "the chav" (Hayward and Yar 2006). It is hardly controversial to note that cultural politics, ideology and economic relations lie at the heart of our current notions of gangs. The gang being a social phenomenon that confirms the dominant world view about how not to live. It is without any redeeming features merely a readily available example of the excesses of degradation and misery of underclass life. From Fagin's gang of urchins through to MS13 the gang is the entity responsible for criminal behaviour in otherwise normal people. It is interesting that criminality is taken as synonymous with gangs. It is commonly understood that one may not just hang out with others, in a gang, because a gang is *intrinsically* criminal (Klein and Maxon 2006, 4). We take from this that the gang is of little interest to the public authorities, other than as something to tirade against. The gang's territory changes, there are variations in the gang's form and in its *modus operandi*, in the clothing, associated music and language, and the drug and criminal markets are in a constant state of change. The micro-ethnography of gangs is, however, of little interest to the public authorities though they may commission research. What really matters about gangs is that they are a ready-made whipping-boy for their own crimes, and by association, the crimes, lifestyles and social conditions of their immediate communities. Recall, *Policing the Crisis* and its demonstration of how the focus upon a narrow form of black criminality, *mugging*, was at root part of a wider assault on black youth and black people in the UK generally (Hall et al. 1978). The lack of any agreed definition of gangs does not undermine the attack on gangs, to say nothing of the huge gang-industry of youth workers and local government officials whose main role is to address the gang and evangelise about its underlying evils. The gang is the *other* for sure. The more it is invoked the more the *nostalgie de la boue* increases: it is in the clothes we all wear, the music we all hear and the television we all watch. How could we live without gangs since they define a whole range of what counts of contemporary life for many of us? In terms of the current literature the gang at first seems somewhat of a mess with everyone starting from different positions and wishing to get to different end points. In truth, the literature falls into certain areas, published by certain journals that share the same basic politics around the gang in terms of its cultural, sociological, public policy and policing significance. In this chapter, I will not be attempting a grand survey of published material or developing a new theory but will note a range of published work and offer a personal response to it. We will focus on two class treatments by Becker and Cohen and recent work by Hardie-Bick, which taken together seem to capture the phenomenon of gangs rather well.

Back to Becker

The gang is defined by its members but more importantly it is defined by those who observe it and note it as *other* (Becker 1963). This is the key insight we have and is given to us by labelling theory. The gang is above all a deviant form. Becker stated that: "Social groups, create deviance by making the rules whose infraction constitutes deviance, and by applying those rules to particular people and labelling them as outsiders. From this point of view, deviance is *not* a quality of the act the person commits but rather a consequence of the application by others of rules and sanctions to an 'offender.' The deviant is one to whom that label has successfully been applied; deviant behaviour is behaviour that people so label" (Becker 1963, 9). Sumner discusses Becker, in some detail, noting how; "What Becker was forging was a sharp break with legalism. His formulations represented a rejection of the view that the law expressed popular morality and was enforced fairly and equally. One could no longer breezily assume that the tenets of the criminal law were an accurate guide to what was legitimately suppressed by authority, or how" (Sumner 1994, 232). What Becker changed for all time was any sense that culture and social setting could ever be peripheral to criminal determination. In this way, he politicised the understanding of gangs for all time. The gang represented a political space and what it does, and does not, do are forever contested. Moreover, writing as he did in the early 1960s, Becker's writings were undertaken during the Civil Rights campaigns of blacks, women, gays and others. The lives of gang members were labelled as deviant by outsiders and their activities similarly defined as criminal by outsiders. This is important since the gang has often been used as the main locus of state interference with working class people; in the United States in the *War on Drugs* and in the UK in terms of anti-social behaviour. Crewe has recently pointed out how Katz and Jackson-Jacobs noted how criminologists themselves were caught up in documenting the gang for the powers that be, and how much of the enterprise of criminological research has been invoked to justify draconian policies against the poor, the disadvantaged and the *other* (Crewe 2016, 1003). Katz and Jackson-Jacobs cite Cloward and Ohlin's work which was used in President Johnson's Great Society War on Poverty which became a war on the poor (Cloward and Ohlin 1960; Katz and Jackson-Jacobs 2004). Elizabeth Hinton's recent book argues, moreover, how the mass incarceration in contemporary America began with well-meaning reforms during the Johnson Administration (Hinton 2016). Returning to Becker, we note how his work *Outsiders* was a key text in labelling theory. Becker's key insight was that *deviance* was not a quality, in itself, but rather was the outcome of someone defining the behaviour of another as wrong, deviant, bad or some such. He looked at the lives of drug users, marijuana smokers, who were seen as deviants in the America of the mid-twentieth century (i.e. they were labelled deviants). He also noted the formation of a deviant culture as a response to this labelling, that individuals could escape the label simply by changing their lifestyles. Deviance being a *constructed* identity it has little ontological inertia. Becker's *Outsiders*, though published in 1963, really made an impact a little later in the sociological tumult that was the 1970s. Becker's work was not technically elaborate nor particularly linked to the key research themes of the era. Becker was, however, a compelling figure and his choice of marijuana and jazz musicians made him more relevant to students at a time when there was a campaign to legalise marijuana and so he was, to some extent, a member of the counter culture of the time. Certainly he was relevant to the lives of many students in a way that other academics had not been. In any case, as Sumner has noted, Becker's work was "uniquely striking" to the sociological audience of the early 1970s (Sumner 1994, 232). Becker focused upon labels and in so doing he stressed the social, and interactive, nature of the labelling process and not the legal definition, *per se*. This is very important since it means that the labellers are independent of the law; that is, their labels are not necessarily based on any legal statute. The law is largely outside of this labelling process and is understood as simply the codified, and rationalised, disapproval of a society of a given activity. Moreover, Becker shows us how *seriousness*, as such, is not what drives labelling. There is no clear graph to be plotted showing any necessary correlation between harm and its public disapproval; all of which explains why marijuana smoking and homosexual activity often receive far greater disapproval than activities that are objectively more serious. If not revolutionary, then Becker's rejection of simple legal formulations, around crime, certainly represented a wholesale refutation of legal populism; or any sense that the law could ever capture the beliefs of the community it served. Becker's labels seem more fleet of foot, more responsive, and certainly more authentic as expressions of popular sentiment than law had been or was ever likely to be. Earlier scholars had thought of crime as a fact of life, inescapable, and as much as they had considered labels, they saw these as an *objective* determination made by the public authorities. Becker did not entirely reject these earlier reflections upon labelling but added to them the understanding that labels had an element of moral and political ideological determination. Moreover, that strictly speaking there can be no deviance without the label. This is not entirely new and to some extent represented a return to Lemert in holding that deviance, or rather judgements about the deviance of others, is crucially about a dispute concerning the priority of values rather than any universal notion embodied within law or even in behaviour (Lemert 1951). Becker took from this that deviance was derived from a deep sense of moral ideology played out politically, as Grant suggests in relation to rioting (Grant 2014). What all this did do, which was revolutionary, was to refocus the study of deviance away from the hitherto dominant themes of its relationship to law and towards an understanding of it in terms of shifting political discourses. The label, was, by implication, a political category and deviants were simply the recipients of ideological determination.

Becker was interested in the fact that people, at different times, contravene laws, breach social taboos and break all manner of rules and regulations but are not labelled as deviant; and other people are labelled as deviant and break no rules or regulations, breach no social taboos or contravene any laws. There is no obvious correlation between criminality or immorality and the label deviant, certainly no clear hierarchy one might map (Oddson and Bernburg 2017). This seems to breach then the prevalent Durkheimian settlement. Becker's position was altogether more haphazard and reasoned that there could never be a clearly articulated rationale for disapproval, censure and condemnation. It is all a matter of the complex interplay of social and political factors coming up with a position within a confused and pluralistic world. People make of things what they will. Becker, unlike the Durkheimians, saw little agreement on matters of whether, or not, a person or group of people were deviant or not (Becker 1963, 8). Becker's *Outsiders* chimed with his era, the 1960s, in noting how the labelling of behaviour was, actually, a matter of whimsy. The hippies, the pot smokers were no worry to anyone and yet they were labelled deviants and the excesses of the elites were brushed aside. One, according to Becker, can discern no obvious relationship between deviance, as a threat to society, and the law. This is a substantial point in terms of justice and something, much later, legal scholars would become fixated on in terms of proportionality in the 1980s and 1990s (von Hirsch 1990, 1996). Becker noted how in trying to understand the operation of deviance we ought to think about it as "…a product of a process which involves responses of other people to the behaviour" (Becker 1963, 14). This is the key sociological insight: deviance is the outcome of the interaction of the actor who undertakes the action and others who react to it. To this extent it is a two-way street and in a later chapter he invokes the analogy of the theatre; the whole thing being somewhat akin to a drama (Becker 1974, 45). All we can make of that is that it places Becker in the symbolic interactionist camp (albeit a politicised one) since all he can say about the nature of deviance is that it is the outcome of the interactions that happen between people and the meanings they ascribe to those inter-actions: in any case, it has a large element of *randomness* built into the model. Although, in other places, Becker suggests that class, race and other variables may play a role in the ascription of deviance to an act or actor (Becker 1963, 12–13). Therefore, if we can account for these vari-ables, such as class and race, the variation may not be as *unmappable* as it seemed at the outset.

Becker understood how society gives rise to different groups and how laws, social conventions and petty rules enable this (Becker 1963, 15). Indeed, one of the features of a modern society is the conflict that arises over rules and rule-based practices and he noted how the struggles, ways of life and resistance of the working classes are often seen as deviant whereas they are merely different responses to social life (Becker 1963, 16). Becker was, of course, pointing not simply to the lack of consensus within the America he found himself in but to the ways experience struc-tures our moral world-view. He noted how black America differs from white America, rural America from urban America, rich from poor and so forth. However, the greatest division is between the understanding of rules; what they are for and who they apply to. There are those who make rules, and in whose interest they are forged, and there are those who are the subject of rules. This is a useful, if fairly obvious, point to make and it was famously criticised by Sumner who noted that: "Becker was not careful enough to resist the fallacy that just because people became devi-ants more from contingency than pathology it did not mean that they were not pathological, rebellious or difficult in some sense. His deviants never seem to have 'an attitude problem' whereas his labellers always had one" (Sumner 1994, 234). We take Sumner's point. All the same, the thrust of Becker's work is surely right to conclude that, generally speak-ing, rules are imposed on the less powerful members of society and the power to exact that settlement resides with those who have the economic and political capacity to ensure it. We note this in small things in our daily lives like when the sixteen-year-old Prince Harry took drugs "at a private party" young men of the same age on the streets of our big cities were being stopped and searched and arrested for the same behaviour (Guardian 12 January 2002). This understanding of how class, race, power and other variables structure rules, legal and conventional, in a differential fashion is at the heart of Becker's analysis. He sees this as part and parcel of modern political life (Becker 1963, 18).

As a result of this social and political settlement around rules, Becker gives us the notion, in *Outsiders*, of *moral enterprise*, in other words the ways in which a rule may be adapted, or changed, and its effect on the way people live. Becker notes how it is a key variable in rule implementation in a world where there is no common agreement on the nature and extent of rules. Becker understands that in these circumstances "if no enterprising person appears, no action is taken" (Becker 1963, 128). Indeed, he maintains that "It is absolutely crucial in the shaping of rules to deal with specific problematic situations" (Becker 1963, 131). Moral enterprise is simply the vehicle whereby values are translated into the conduct of our everyday lives. It also shows up Becker's politics, since we reason how deviance is likely to be oppositional and at odds with the dominant legal and moral sentiments of the age. The moral entrepreneur is therefore key to the way that deviance comes to be understood. Moral entrepreneurs can reject the dominant legal and moral sentiments of their age. Becker's marijuana smokers did this but so do gays, women and youth on the streets. Becker noted how deviance, on these grounds, is "always the result of enterprise" (Becker 1963, 162). He understood how the rules had to originally be formulated and then someone had to apply them. As Sumner expressed it: "It involves a continual reinforcement, restatement, reform or re-representation of the practical meaning of society's most powerful moral codes and political/economic interests" (Sumner 1994, 236). This is the important point to take from Becker; that deviance and deviance-labelling is an intrinsically political activity. In developing the work of earlier scholars, Becker opened the possibility of reconceiving the deviant, not as a wastrel or a ne'er do well or a rogue, but as a person implicated in a form of social resistance. In this regard, Becker remains of crucial importance to the task of understanding the gang. Whatever else the gang is it is certainly implicated in the *to and fro* of rule setting and resistance. Gangs represent a form of deviance with its own norms and values and Becker neatly sets out a readily understandable political and social landscape in which to contextualise them and a lens with which to look at how the gang may undertake a role in the social construction of rules, and their resistance. He was an advocate of ethnography making it clear that: "The researcher, therefore, must participate intensively and continuously with the deviants he wants to study so that they will get to know him well enough to be able to make some assessment of whether his activities will adversely affect theirs" (Becker 1963, 168). This is an aspect of Becker's methodology that has been taken up by cultural criminologists, along with his idea of *cool* which is now taken up as important area of study around gangs and the broader set of issues that relate to street life (Ilan 2015). Moreover, Becker was undoubtedly on the side of the underdog and politically committed to a liberal politics and to this extent remains both an inspiration and at times an active ingredient in much of the Critical Criminology that followed, and his notion of the moral entrepreneur was picked up by Stan Cohen.

Stan Cohen: Real Issues and Constructed Issues

Cohen's contribution right across the Social Sciences is characterised by it breadth and by its depth. He made substantial contributions to scholarship in human rights, legal and political theory, and the study of modern media. However, it is his *Folk Devils and Moral Panics* (1973) and, crucially, his idea of the *moral panic* that is of key importance to the study of gangs. We note also how *Folk Devils and Moral Panics* set out the ground for other important work, notably *Policing the Crisis: Mugging, the State and Law and Order* (1978) by Hall et al., which famously exposed the moral panic around "mugging" which was built upon the linkage of race, black youth and crime by the media and the public authorities. Cohen wanted to build on the work of Becker by noting a deviancy amplification through a structured media distortion that gave rise to a moral panic. Cohen was part of the awkward squad and aligned to the National Deviancy Conference (NDC). His work was, like that of Jock Young, interested in the conflicts that arise between so-called deviant groups and the voices raised against them (Cohen 1971). Cohen, like Becker, was never taken with a statistical basis for his work, legal statute or the analysis of policy

(Amatrudo and Blake 2015, 6). Cohen, like Becker, seemed to align himself *somewhat* with the deviants he studied and so maybe he is open to Sumner's criticism, of Becker, that he is in danger of understanding their deviance as entirely constructed by others and having, itself, no substantive reality (Sumner 1994, 234). I think we can acquit Cohen of falling into this fallacy, but nonetheless it should be noted that in looking at one side of the equation a little more keenly than the other leaves open the possibility of partisanship. Moreover, Cohen's use of language, *folk devils*, leaves the reader in no doubt that there is a hint of glamour here, a touch of romance; after all the subject of study is the everyday lives of young people and the setting the everyday working-class spaces they inhabit. Cohen's work, far more so than with Becker, relates directly to the role of ideology and, what became a defining theme in his work, social control. Before looking more closely at *Folk Devils and Moral Panics* it is useful to take a look at his *Visions of Social Control: Crime, Punishment and Classification* (1985) since it will give a more rounded view of Cohen's work.

Cohen sets out in *Visions of Social Control: Crime, Punishment and Classification* how since the nineteenth century there has been an increase in the differentiation, and classification, of deviant groups and dependent groups each with its own separate system of knowledge and accredited experts; and how the state is implicated in this (Cohen 1985,12). This view overlaps with the work of Foucault and Rusche and Kirchheimer. Cohen held that the capitalist system requires newer, more consistent and harsher mechanisms of social control. Moreover, that the entire enterprise of social control was directed not simply at criminals, or deviants, but at the working class, in general, with the aim of producing a passive, and compliant, population. He noted how: "It renders docile the recalcitrant members of the working class. It deters others, it teaches habits of discipline and order, and it reproduces the lost hierarchy. It repairs defective humans to compete in the marketplace" (Cohen 1985, 23). The notion that social control though superficially aimed at criminals and deviants is aimed at a much bigger target, the working class is a very important insight. Police action against gangs may understood not simply as a response to criminality but also in terms of the chilling function it has on youth, the working class, and historically, in the UK, the black community in general (Hallsworth and Young 2008). Interestingly, in thinking about the mechanisms of social control in these terms Cohen invokes Durkheim in terms of "… boundary maintenance, rule classification, social solidarity" (Cohen 1985, 233). In *Visions of Social Control: Crime, Punishment and Classification* Cohen points away from the *immediate*, to employ Jock Young's term, and towards more profound moral sentiments about the way we live together in a post-modern society. He notes how the system of social control grows, over time, and famously shows how the net is widened and the mesh is thinned (Cohen 1985). Allied to moral panic is the mechanism of social control and Cohen shows us that a "…choice between exclusion and inclusion is, above all else, a political decision determined by the nature of the state. Nevertheless, different as the actual governing criterion is, the dimensions of choice at each stage of the system are the same. At the macro-level, do we construct exclusive or inclusive systems? At the micro-level do we exclude or include this particular individual?" (Cohen 1985, 271). We must always understand that when we read Cohen we are reading an activist who had far more in mind that simple ethnography, his concerns were profoundly political.

If we look at *Folk Devils and Moral Panics* we see how Cohen was following a well-trodden

Durkheimian path in terms of conceiving of the moral panic as a *voluntary* aspect of all societies along with the underlying connection between the object of the panic, the deviant, and those who disapproved and disparaged. One notes also a reliance upon Marxist social theory, in order to say something more meaningful about the nature of class and of power. More controversially, we may follow Sumner in seeing that a "… psychoanalytic use of the term panic, was located at the collective level" (Sumner 1994, 264). There is certainly a complexity, and lack of purity, in Cohen's work on moral panic. He was bold enough to take elements, and insights, from a range of Schools, thinkers and approaches. Since we are addressing the matter of gangs then the element that has most resonance, in terms of *moral panic*, is the notion of what Cohen termed *deviancy amplification*. In the case of *Folk Devils and Moral Panics* Cohen looks at the mods and rockers phenomenon. These two youth subcultures would get into fights, often at English seaside resorts. The mods were moderns and saw themselves as, supposedly, socially progressive and aspirational. They wore smart clothes and rode Italian scooters. They listened to bands like the Small Faces and the Who and Motown music from the United States and they liked dancing and taking amphetamines. The rockers were, supposedly, more socially conservative than the mods, they wore denim jeans and leather jackets and rode around on BSA, Norton and Triumph motorcycles. They listened to rock and roll music but they were not so keen on dancing. These two groups were represented as embodying social and political values that were at odds with each other and in this they represented very real conflicts at the heart of civic life. However, their skirmishes were actually quite minor; and the level of delinquency was hyped up as was the outrage to it. Cohen was keen to explore the symbolic importance of the clothes, the music and the two-wheeled transport and how it was related to a mass audience through the media. This was not entirely novel but as Sumner has noted: "Cohen's combination of Durkheim, the 1930s vision of cultural irrationality, symbolic interactionism, the class contradictions within the leisure culture of the welfare state, the signifying power of the modern mass media, and an acute awareness of the general significance of the Mod, effected a renewed expression of the most penetrating features of modernist analysis" (Sumner 1994, 265).

Cohen was very important in promulgating the notion that the media were key to understanding the way moral panic operates. Although he was not the first to do so, Cohen noted how the media have an important role in processing information before it is consumed (Cohen 1973, 16). He also noted how the media have a need to engage and entertain their audience and in focusing upon the real-life drama of deviance they inevitably amplified the perceived level of deviancy and tended to seek to protect existing political and social values (Cohen 1973, 138). Cohen afforded a major role in the process of amplification through a continuous process of defining, denouncing and then amplifying the level of deviancy that they drew to their audience's attention. Moreover, with such a powerful, and probably imprecise, media coverage and given that the so-called deviants will inevitably respond to it in kind, it follows that a gap will, almost certainly, open up between the social reality of the situation and the players concerned and the distorted media representation of it. In this way, Cohen saw the media as creating a distance between the world as it is and the way the world is represented. He understood how this was exacerbated by matters of media ownership and the existence of an entrenched morality that was loath to change. Cohen also understood how this process would become something of a game and that the deviants too would become unclear or, worse still, the deviants would be wrongly ordered. He noted how white-collar criminality, and complex criminality, tends to be hardly examined unlike the more readily understood lives of the young, blacks, Muslims, gays, demonstrators, for example, who are regularly cited as threats to law and order. One notes a similarity with the work of his contemporary, Jock Young, here and they did collaborate (Cohen and Young 1973). The important point Cohen, and Young, noted was that this distorting deviancy amplification was essentially a modern phenomenon and how it was focused upon reinforcing the existing moral and political settlement through a process of stigmatisation of those elements in society thought a threat, whether they were, or not. Cohen's genius was in understanding how all of this soon settles down and that: "Action gets restructured around the familiar settings of streets, sports grounds, the weekend by the sea, railway station. The settings are given new meanings by being made stages for these games" (Cohen 1973, 53). It all becomes an everyday and unremarkable aspect of all our lives (Brotherton 2015, 34–35). Moreover, as this process settles down and takes hold there arises a "… symbolic and linguistic loop which involves a range of mutually reinforcing social actors, media workers, politicians, social workers, social scientists, teachers, police and civil servants" (Brotherton 2015, 120). Cohen's work is easily understood, empirically verifiable and compelling which is what he still inspires.

Hardie-Bick: Self-uncertainty, Violence and Gang Membership

Becker and Cohen are giant figures but there is a new, and growing, body of work that takes inspiration from the philosophical and psychoanalytical writings of Erich Fromm and the, more recent, psychological work of

Michael Hogg. They argue that modern people employ *escape* mechanisms to protect them from the estrangement and insecurity of contemporary life. Hogg has developed what he terms an uncertainty-identity theory. Hardie-Bick has recently sought to combine the psychoanalytical insights with Hogg's more existential uncertainty-identity theory in order to explain the violent and destructive behaviour of groups (Hardie-Bick 2016). This work represents both a challenge to existing *gang-talk* (Hallsworth and Young 2008) and offers a new set of issues for scholars to ponder (Reiner 2016, 196–197). The work makes explicit reference to existential themes and shares some of Cohen's political savvyness. It is compatible with cultural criminological scholarship, which itself has been touched by an interest in philosophical explanation (Ilan 2015). The focus on existential thought is in terms of looking at social reality being constructed out of indeterminacy and ambiguity and modern life itself being understood as anxiety-inducing. This attention upon existential thought is part of a body of work, within criminological theory, that has gained currency in the past decade (Lippens and Crewe 2009). The question Hardie-Bick sets himself in his essay "Escaping the Self: Identity, Group Identification and Violence" is very germane to the topic of gangs: it is the question of why people choose to give up their individuality. Interestingly, Hardie-Bick looks for an answer in the work of Erich Fromm, who was a scholar of authoritarianism and social conformity; and especially his *Escape from Freedom* which was originally written in 1941. In using Fromm, Arrigo and Williams have noted that the argument is:

"...targeted toward the capitalistic mode of production, the industrial and technological means by which it functioned and new psychological states and social relations it therefore produced. On the one hand, capitalism established a heightened personal independence expressed through 'individualistic activity,' Indeed, capitalism not only freed (us) from traditional (feudal) bonds, but it also contributed tremendously to the increasing of positive freedom, to the growth of an active, critical, responsible self. This sense of autonomy and freedom' put the individual entirely on his (or her) own feet, advancing the growth 'process of individualization' .... On the other hand, the effect of capitalism fostered isolation, fear, and loneliness for the ostensibly self-made citizen, imbuing the person with a feeling of insignificance and powerlessness" (Arrigo and Williams 2009, 231).

Allied to this Hardie-Bick utilises the work of Michael Hogg, which notes a connection between what he terms "self-uncertainty" and subsequent group identification; understanding that there is an important relationship between these two variables (Hogg 2007, 2014).

What Hardie-Bick argues is that psychological and sociological factors embedded within modernity make people "…increasingly independent and critical, but at the same time more isolated and insecure" (Hardie-Bick 2016, 1035). This argument is built on Fromm's belief that our primary bonds, that is the sorts of social, and emotional, bonds that existed in pre-modern societies and produced a clear sense of order and identity, largely dictating family membership and place, are undermined by modern living. This inevitably causes insecurity since the bonds that gave people a sense of belonging have largely disappeared. Accordingly, without these necessary bonds people seem isolated, unempowered and insecure. Fromm saw how modern life could be characterised, in many ways, by the pursuit of new, *secondary*, bonds to replace the primary ones and give back a sense of security and well-being to people (Fromm 1941). "They have no desire, want, or urge to set goals and engage in pro-attitudinal thinking and to begin to act in a way directed at positive outcomes" (Amatrudo 2015a, b, 979). The sort of landscape that Fromm maps out is fertile ground for existentialist reflection and certainly many, notably Camus, Heidegger and Sartre, have followed this vein. Hardie-Bick particularly stresses the work of Sartre and notes how, for some, the responsibility for living a good life, a life in which one creates one's own values, is not something they welcome at all; indeed, it is stress inducing. As contemporary sociologists, such as Bauman and Beck, have argued, the modern life is a risky and precarious life (Beck 1998). The loss of traditional ways of living and the dissolution of many of the things that gave one certainty, as the way we conceive gender and class position, is anxiety-inducing; it offers people incompleteness and a lack of focus (Bauman 2000). These issues are also noted in the work of the social psychologist, Michael Hogg, in his work on uncertainty-identity theory. Hogg regards inter-group conflict as developing differentiated identities as groups define *against* one another. Hogg's notion is that feelings of uncertainty are crucial in the understanding of how, and why, attachment to a group comes about (Hogg 2007). It is uncertainty that forces people to engage in behaviour that reduces uncertainty and that group membership serves to reduce social anxiety and uncertainty, and increases self-esteem (Hogg 2014). Uncertainty-identity theory examines these processes in terms of assuaging social anxiety (Hardie-Bick 2016, 1037). Hogg puts it clearly: "We are particularly motivated to reduce uncertainty if, in a particular context, we feel uncertain about things that reflect on or are relevant to self, or if we are uncertain about self, *per se*; about our identity, who are, how we relate to others, and how to behave and what to think, and who others are and how they might behave and what they might think" (Hogg 2007, 73). In developing a strong sense of identity, the individual is protected from uncertainty and anxiety. If they are unable to achieve this then feelings of uncertainty, anxiety and threat emerge, and this leads to a sense of existential uncertainty within the individual.

The identification with a group is crucially about reducing the uncertainty and anxiety that are a feature of contemporary life. However, this identification with a group is not a straightforward good because in expressing identity this can bring about intergroup conflict. Sen has argued that the flip-side of group affiliation is social tension and violence (Sen 2006, 21). This dilemma of group membership was taken up by Jock Young as the sense of belonging individuals have as part of a group is "… inevitably accompanied (by the) denigration of the other" (Young 2007, 141). Hogg, and Young, understood this Janus-faced nature of group membership as both an escape from existential anxiety and a cause of it. The drive to join a group and gain the benefits of social solidarity and a stronger sense of self-identity is also implicated in the rationale for joining terrorist groups (Cottee and Hayward 2011, 973). The same is true of street gangs where, if anything, the relationship between self-uncertainty and joining a group is clearer. Yet rather than think of gangs in terms of social disorganisation or any number of other reasons we would do better to see how uncertainty-identity theory better maps the street gang against the existential needs of individuals and explains why some people leave gangs whilst other continue with their affiliation. "The (two) most significant explanations for the attractions of gang member-ship. First of all, they claim that young people are attracted to join gangs for social reasons. For example, they may have a friend or family member who is already involved with a gang. Secondly, they suggest that many youth believe they will be protected and feel safer if they join a gang" (Hardie-Bick 2016, 1039). Once in a gang, membership often entails anxiety-inducing illegal, often violent, behaviour. The dangers are weighed against the sense of social solidarity. Moreover, Hogg has argued that those people with the highest levels of social anxiety and weak levels of personal identity are precisely the sorts of people likely to join a group with a rigid sense of identity, *sic* certainty. Hogg notes how, over time, our society has become increasingly atomised. He notes: "By the 1950s, these stable identities had been almost entirely replaced by a more atomistic individual-oriented status society ... producing the postmodern paradox in which people with today's less structured self yearn for community and the collective affiliations of past times" (Hogg 2007, 93–94).

If we return to Fromm's *Escape from Freedom* we note that authoritari-anism is one vehicle for escaping the uncertainty of modern life as people become automatons in a larger mechanism. Individuals give up their freedom and independence and fuse their identity with the larger group-ing. We note this in Fascist politics but also, in a different form, in the life of the gang where the individual becomes insignificant when weighed against the collective. Moreover, members of the group come to see other in this way, not as individual but as members, like them. This, it has been argued, makes violence easier since it is about members not real people with real lives. It is certainly a compelling and readily understood notion. What Hardie-Bick points us towards is a highly sophisticated model of human behaviour to explain gangs and gang activity. "A firm sense of belonging can also lead to the denigration, humiliation and dehu-manisation of others who do not share their own in-group identity" (Hardie-Bick 2016, 1046). The approach Hardie-Bick advocates incor-porates both sociological and psychological insight and is built on a solid philosophical base. It elegantly addresses both the rationale for joining a gang in readily understood social-psychological terms and offers an expla-nation as to why gang members are willing to engage in risky behaviour; risky that is to themselves.

Conclusion

As I pointed out at the outset, *the gang* has had a great deal of time devoted to it. In any case, it is a complex topic and a multi-faceted phenomenon and it is unlikely there will ever be a single approach that will give us the ability to understand it completely. There is no unified theory of gangs. That said, it is certainly possible to highlight approaches likely to be useful. In looking at the gang in terms of the work of Becker and Cohen, and in terms of the more existential fashion Hardie-Bick suggests, we will plant our quest for understanding in rich, substantial and proven intellectual soil. Moreover, these three approaches are compatible. They simple look at different features of the gang and its genesis. These three positions are compatible and mutually reinforcing.

In using Becker, we note that the gang is, in many ways, a label, a social construction. Becker taught us to reject the naïve view that law is simply the expression of popular morality. He explained how law is neither fair nor equally enforced. He showed us how both culture and social setting are crucial to understanding the process of criminalisation. In this way, he politicised the gang and the life of the gang. He noted how once labelled as outsiders, by outsiders, gang members became exactly that, outsiders. The label alters the behaviour of people, no less gang members. The gang becomes a site of state activity against the working class generally, not just gang members. We note this in London in the application of stop and search tactics by the police, supposedly targeted at gangs but, in practice, that has historically meant local working-class, often black, youths. The same is true in the United States in the *War on Drugs* which has meant a concentration upon inner-city communities, as much as on gangs. We also note how this slippage from gang to local community may be no incidental issue. Becker shows us how deviant culture is often a response to the labelling of others. It is the result of the moral and political ideological determination of others. There is no deviance without the labelling of the deviant. Therefore, the label is a political category and deviants are simply the recipients of this *external* ideological determination. This ideological determination shifts over time and labels different people at different times but the important thing to note in Becker is the political nature of the labelling process and how there is no necessary cor-relation between seriousness, immorality, social threat or anything else with the ideological determination of the labeller. Moreover, he tells us that deviance itself is the outcome of a drama, of action and reaction with certain variables amplifying the reaction (Becker 1963, 12–13). He noted how modern society throws up conflicts over rules and how resistance, *sic* deviance, is implicated in that. He noted how the most important thing of note in the conflict over rule setting was who determined the rules, for whom, and who are subject to them. The power to impose rules is the power to marginalise others and to label them deviant, against a standard set by the powerful. In Becker, gangs represent a form of resistance on one level, and on another, they are groups that also set their own norms and values. Becker was undoubtedly supportive of the weaker members of society and understood the nature of power and the expressive func-tion of the label. This did not mean he approved of all the activities of the gang only that as a sociologist he understood the way a gang was con-structed and formed out of an unfair social setting.

In Cohen's work, we see how deviance is amplified through the media to cause a moral panic. He followed Becker in noting how social control was not simply aimed at criminals but at the wider working class. He famously noted: "It renders docile the recalcitrant members of the work-ing class. It deters others, it teaches habits of discipline and order, and it reproduces the lost hierarchy. It repairs defective humans to compete in the marketplace" (Cohen 1985, 23). He was far ahead of his time in not-ing how police campaigns, ostensibly against gangs, had a chilling effect on the communities that those gang members came from and, in the UK, this has often meant an over-concentration on black populations. Cohen's moral panics may also be understood as strengthening the bonds of con-nectedness between denouncers, as it is a mechanism for promulgating popular morality. In *Folk Devils and Moral Panics*, Cohen looks the mods and rockers in the 1960s which he understood as archetypal of certain values and therefore their skirmishes were, at heart, a battle between cer-tain social values. What Cohen was keen to do was to explain how the media conveyed how these mods and rockers lived their lives, set up the moral panic and then amplified its significance in a way that both enter-tains and upholds *traditional* moral values. He showed how this process of fermenting a moral panic and then amplifying its importance is necessarily both distorting and distraction from far more important social and political ills.

The work Hardie-Bick highlights is interesting for a variety of reasons. It points us to the drive for social acceptance and certainty and illustrates the ontological insecurity of the contemporary world. It also roots the insights of Becker and Cohen in the philosophical and psychoanalytical writings of Erich Fromm and the, more recent, psychological work of Michael Hogg and others. Hogg's uncertainty-identity theory seems fruitful as does the understanding of a social reality being constructed out of indeterminacy and ambiguity. It is surely true that modern life is anxiety-inducing, especially for those at the margins. It is easy to understand the progression from self-uncertainty to group identification (Hogg 2014). Likewise, the pull of the supposed security of the group for the socially isolated living, as they do, in a risky and precarious social and economic world. We understand how groups define against themselves; Cohen said as much. However, we note too that group membership also comes with its own rules and it too can generate anxiety in its members (Hardie-Bick 2016, 1037). Street gangs are vehicles for the socially insecure and self-uncertain to come together. The gang satisfies an existential need in its members. The dangers of gang membership, which include incarceration and being the victim of physical violence, are weighed against the sense of social solidarity they provide. The less structured the lives of individuals, the more they crave structure and social solidarity. The rise of gangs in our inner cities somewhat correlates with this process (Hogg 2007, 93–94). When people join gangs, they think of themselves as gang members not as individuals, *per se*. Hardie-Bick explains why people join gangs and go on to engage in risky behaviour, and sets out ways to understand this.

Bibliography

Amatrudo, A. (2015a). Unheimlichkeit: Alienated and Integrated Identities and Criminal Existence(s). *Law, Jurisprudence, Governance and Existential Indeterminacy: Onati Socio-Legal Series, 5*(3), 969–981.

Amatrudo, A. (2015b). Individuals and Groups of Individuals Breaking Laws. In D. Crewe & R. Lippens (Eds.), *What is Criminology About?* (pp. 105–122). Abingdon: Routledge.

Amatrudo, A., & Blake, L. (2015). *Human Rights and the Criminal Justice System*. London: Routledge.

Arrigo, B., & Williams, C. (2009). Existentialism and the Criminology of the Shadow. In R. Lippens & D. Crewe (Eds.), *Existentialist Criminology* (pp. 222–245). London: Routledge.

Bauman, Z. (2000). *Liquid Modernity*. Cambridge: Polity Press.

Beck, U. (1998). *Risk Society: Towards a New Modernity*. London: Sage.

Becker, H. (1963). *Outsiders*. New York: Free Press.

Becker, H. (1974). Labelling Theory Reconsidered. In P. Rock & M. McIntosh (Eds.), *Deviance and Social Control*. London: Tavistock Press.

Bowling, B., & Phillips, C. (2007). Disproportionate and Discriminatory: Reviewing the Evidence on Police Stop and Search. *Modern Law Review, 70*(6), 936–961.

Brotherton, D. (2007). Beyond Social Reproduction: Bringing Resistance Back Into the Theory of Gangs. *Theoretical Criminology, 12*(1), 55–77.

Brotherton, D. (2015). *Youth Street Gangs: A Critical Appraisal*. London: Routledge.

Cloward, R., & Ohlin, L. (1960). *Delinquency and Opportunity: A Theory of Delinquent Gangs*. New York: Free Press.

Cohen, S. (1971). *Images of Deviance*. Harmondsworth: Penguin Books.

Cohen, S. (1973). *Folk Devils and Moral Panics*. St Albans: Paladin Press.

Cohen, S. (1985). *Visons of Social Control: Crime, Punishment and Classification*. Cambridge: Polity Press.

Cohen, S., & Young, J. (1973). *The Manufacture of News: Deviance, Social Problems and the Mass Media*. London: Constable.

Cotte, S., & Hayward, K. (2011). The Terrorist (E)Motives: The Existential Attractions of Terrorism. *Studies in Conflict and Terrorism, 34*(12), 963–986.

Crewe, D. (2013). *Becoming Criminal: The Socio-Cultural Origins of Law, Transgression and Deviance*. Basingstoke: Palgrave Macmillan.

Crewe, D. (2016). Gang: Culture, Eidos and Process. *The Politics and Jurisprudence of Group Offending: Onati Socio-Legal Series, 6*(4), 999–1015.

Fromm, E. (1941). *Escape From Freedom*. New York: Henry Holt & Company.

Grant, J. (2014). Riots in the UK: Morality, Social Imaginaries and Conditions of Possibility. *New Political Science, 36*(3), 311–329.

Hall, S., et al. (1978). *Policing the Crisis: Mugging, the State, and Law and Order*. London: Macmillan.

Hallsworth, S. (2013). *The Gang and Beyond: Interpreting Violent Street Worlds*. London: Palgrave Macmillan.

Hallsworth, S., & Young, T. (2008). Gang Talk and Gang Talkers. *Crime, Media and Culture, 4*(2), 175–195.

Hardie-Bick, J. (2016). Escaping the Self: Identity, Group Identification and Violence. *The Politics and Jurisprudence of Group Offending: Onati Socio-Legal Series, 6*(4), 1032–1052.

Hayward, K., & Yar, M. (2006). The 'Chav' Phenomenon: Consumption, Media and the Construction of a New Underclass. *Crime, Media and Culture, 2*(1), 9–28.

Hinton, E. (2016). *From the War on Poverty to the War on Crime: The Making of Mass Incarceration in America*. Cambridge: Harvard University Press.

von Hirsch, A. (1990). The Politics of Just Deserts. *Canadian Journal of Criminology, 397*(32), 407–409.

von Hirsch, A. (1996). *Censure and Sanctions*. Oxford: Clarendon Press.

Hogg, M. (2007). Uncertainty-Identity Theory. *Advances in Experimental Social Psychology, 39*(1), 69–126.

Hogg, M. (2014). From Uncertainty to Extremism: Social Categorization and Identity Processes. *Current Directions in Psychological Science, 23*(5), 338–342.

Ilan, J. (2015). *Understanding Street Culture: Poverty, Crime, Youth and Cool*. London: Palgrave Macmillan.

Jacques, S., & Wright, R. (2015). *Code of the Suburb: Inside the World of Young Middle-Class Drug Dealing*. Chicago: Chicago University Press.

Katz, J., & Jackson-Jacobs, C. (2004). The Criminologist's Gang. In C. Sumner (Ed.), *Blackwell Companion to Criminology* (pp. 91–124). Oxford: Blackwell.

Klein, M., & Maxon, C. (2006). *Street Gang Patterns and Policies*. Oxford: OUP.

Lemert, E. (1951). *Social Pathology*. New York: McGraw-Hill.

Lippens, R., & Crewe, D. (2009). *Existentialist Criminology*. London: Routledge.

Mayeda, D., Chesney-Lind, M., & Koo, J. (2001). Talking Story with Hawaii's Youth: Confronting Violent and Sexualized Perceptions of Ethnicity and Gender. *Youth and Society, 33*(1), 99–128.

Oddson, G., & Bernburg, J. (2017). Opportunity Beliefs and Class Differences in Subjective Status Injustice During the Great Icelandic Recession. *Acta Sociologica*. Published Online First: July 2017.

Panfil, V. (2014). Better Left Unsaid? The Role of Agency in Queer Criminological Research. *Critical Criminology, 22*(1), 99–111.

Reiner, R. (2016). *Crime*. Cambridge: Polity Press.

Sen, A. (2006). *Identity and Violence: The Illusion of Destiny*. New York: Norton.

Squires, P. (2016). *Voodoo Liability*: Joint Enterprise Prosecution as an Aspect of Intensified Criminalisation. *The Politics and Jurisprudence of Group Offending: Onati Socio-Legal Series, 6*(4), 937–956.

Sumner, C. (1994). *The Sociology of Deviance: An Obituary*. Buckingham: Open University Press.

Young, J. (2007). *The Vertigo of Late Modernity*. London: Sage.

7

Drawing the Strands Together

This book is comprised of three sections: technical and analytical considerations, legal considerations, and reality and sociology. The idea of addressing the topic by means of sections itself is an admission of the complexity of the matters at hand when dealing with social aspects of crime. Technical and analytical considerations are markedly absent in the contemporary criminological literature. It is not uncommon for criminologists to take street gangs, for example, as a given and then to go on and conflate gang membership with criminal activity as though the two are synonymous (Pyrooz et al. 2016, 365–397). This has led to some very bad work, both in the academic and policy arenas, especially in relation to black and working class youth (Smithson et al. 2013). In Chap. 1 we examined the complex determination of collective action and in Chap. 2 we examined collective goal setting and arriving at a common goal, something of vital importance when determining legal responsibility. These are technical considerations but they are crucial to the determination of culpability in group offending cases, especially in the light of the abuses of joint enterprise prosecutions in the UK (Squires 2016). It is important for justice that it is established whether or not individuals are involved in a genuine collective action and the same holds for establishing the goals

© The Author(s) 2018
A. Amatrudo, *Criminal Actions and Social Situations*,
https://doi.org/10.1057/978-1-137-45731-8_7

individuals have in mind. There is a great deal of published work on gangs and other jointly authored crimes, along with organised crime, but this is pretty much cut off from technical discussions about social ontology, and contemporary criminological research overlooks pertinent work in law, philosophy and political theory. What we require is a far more nuanced, and philosophically more rigorous, account of persons and the groups they belong to in the context of intentional action, goal setting and responsibility. The street gang itself is over-determined in a great deal of the criminological literature, often without much evidence for this over-determination. Moreover, this over-determination is often accompanied by what can only be termed "sensationalist" writing, one might even say it amounts to a reactionary moral panic (Harding 2014). It is important when we assess the nature of groups that we meticulously work through the relationships to establish the nature of individual and collective actions and the nature of any collective goals. Criminology must relate, and fairly immediately, to the criminal law. Criminologists are centrally concerned with criminals, not with youths or gangs, *per se*. Criminality must be established: it cannot be assumed. Hitherto, criminologists have taken groups as straightforward associations and neglected the technical, and problematic, issues of how intention and action structures membership and action. They also tend to overlook the fleeting nature of many groups, notably street gangs, and overstate the continuity of group membership over time. It is a legacy of the history of sociological writing that interactionism remains hugely influential, especially in relation to the understanding of street gangs. This is not altogether a bad thing, but interactionism tends to argue that it is primarily through interaction that persons, and groups of people, define their context and go on to assign meanings. This approach allows for a great deal of social change and it obviously prioritises the role of culture, but it also tends to work with a sense that there is an underlying stability to the person. In other words, though the meanings and the contexts fluctuate, the person doing the changing is largely unexamined. We also note how interactionists conceive of groups as *essentially* defined by the nature of their interactions, and not the nature of their intentions. This is a very unsophisticated approach existentially. It completely ignores work by philosophers, such as Bratman (1999) and Gilbert (2000), and, in terms of contemporary political theory, List and Petit (2011) with their emphasis upon the role of social ontology, collective action and goal setting. In general, the treatment of the street gang, for example, tends to overplay its homogeneity, understanding it as a super-individual. This also understates how individuals are themselves understandable, in many ways, as mini-associations. In neglecting intentionality, there is a tendency to somewhat conflate, or put on the same ontological footing, armed robbers with their loose bonds and heightened sense of intention with street gangs who may well have tight social bonds but who also exhibit a diminished sense of intention. Interactionism ascribes intentionality all too easily and so is liable to overdetermine the ontological status of groups. Personal identity is based on the psychological connectedness between intentional episodes or person-stages (Parfit 1984). A continuous person is an association between intentions, desires and beliefs at different points in time. Criminology needs to think more in terms of coming up with a form of explanation better able to differentiate action and intentional states: thereby, saying something meaningful about the *criminal* responsibility of individuals and groups.

The aim of criminology must be to reorientate itself, especially in areas such as joint criminal enterprise, in terms of a far more expanded notion of *individual action*, as the basis for legal responsibility and away from reductive collectivist accounts. When this is done the matter of culpability appears far clearer. This is necessary because law is concerned with the *wilful* action of people. The sort of thing I have in mind is illustrated by the treatment of war criminals where there is an over-emphasis upon the structural situation of the individual, as opposed to his, or her, role in criminal action. Although, I readily concede that the place a person occupies in an organisation, or in a social group, has obvious implications for their likely actions, and that this is of importance to investigators. I also hold that membership of a proscribed organisation may itself be culpable. The main point, however, is surely that culpability primarily relates to the actions of individuals (and groups made up of individuals) and in this sense it is not a structural, or ontological, matter. This holds true whether we are discussing war criminals, bank robbers, rioters or street gangs. The person who wields the knife is surely more culpable that the fellow traveller in the gang. Moreover, the issue of deliberation, goal setting and intentionality cannot be marginalised. In understanding how persons act in groups and set goals together and deliberate, we understand criminal action far better. There is a need to deconstruct many of the taken for granted arguments advanced in the understanding of criminal action by using technical tools. In the case of joint criminal enterprise, for example, the claim that persons are acting in unison, or with common purpose, is a very complex determination. I am not claiming that collective action is impossible, only that it is a complicated determination and, in any case, it must be established instead of assumed. Collective action can happen, but persons can also self-impose constraints upon their own thoughts and actions and these self-impositions take the form of intentions and goals: however, these self-impositions do not convey, necessarily, any normative force. Collective action *only* occurs when each of a set of persons adopts the same set of constraints upon their personal thoughts and actions, in order that *they* are committed to bringing about some element of a common set of collectively acceptable outcomes. This view is essentially individualistic and notes all persons deliberating and goal setting themselves, though within the context of a group. It cannot be sub-contracted to the street gang, or some such group. Collective goals nonetheless imply the individual moral agency of individuals in a group. The technical and analytical considerations examined in the first two chapters may be hard work, and largely new to a criminological audience, but they are nonetheless necessary for a more radical, and more realistic, account of criminal actions in social settings.

Persons who face a decision problem can engage in a variety of types of reasoning. In the criminal law, this reasoning relates directly to matters of culpability. To rationally engage in cooperative reasoning with others, a person must rationally hold a collective goal, and they must also reason about which action, or actions, to perform in the light of the collective goal that they possess, with others. The task of goal setting and whether those goals are action intentions or outcome intentions is extremely important to subsequent issues, in our case, criminal liability. These goals necessarily constrain a person's deliberation. Collective goals constrain the deliberation of *every* actor in the collective, not just some of them. Collective goals are equivalent to outcome intentions since they are intentions to bring about some particular outcome, or set of particular outcomes. It is sufficient to note here that any collective goal an actor has is held *assuming* the other parties to it hold it likewise. We can hold that the actor who possesses the collective goal believes that there is a common belief among the actors in the collective about what the collective, i.e. group, consists of. The actor believes that there are common beliefs about the structure of the decision problem in goal setting. We looked at the issue of multi-party decision-making problems (MPDMP) in some detail. We understood that actors not only need to share a common goal but they must reason the best way to bring it about and how to coordinate with one another to bring about the collectively intended outcome. This sort of reasoning seems appropriate in determining the level of culpability an individual, in a group, has in an action. It is therefore appropriate to determining criminal culpability; and far safer than assuming it with imprecise tools as with joint criminal enterprise prosecutions.

In the second section of the book we looked at the legal considerations that flow from treating people as part of a group, wider than themselves, especially in respect to responsibility: in other words, determining where to place responsibility—with the group or with the individual—and on what basis. We looked at the policing of demonstrations where the police, on the ground, have the thankless task of distinguishing between good and bad protestors, and are expected to balance individual rights to protest against matters of order and public safety in difficult and fast-moving situations. We noted how the crowd was, of its nature, a heterogeneous form and how the public have always been suspicious of it, notably in the eighteenth and nineteenth centuries (Rude 1964; rua Wall 2016). In addressing the police tactic of kettling, we noted how in some public order situations treating individuals primarily as group members, instead of simply as autonomous persons, is a practical public order decision. By looking at a sample of court cases we noted the complex task the law must achieve in the area of public order. We made explicit reference to Harding's tripartite model of action (Harding 2007, 81–82). (1) *Human Individual Action* as a straightforward way to assess "interpersonal relations, when the individual's identity as such is a governing dynamic" (Harding 2007, 81). (2) *Individuals Acting Collectively as a Group.* This shows us how individuals can both be part of a group and yet retain their individual "identity as individuals remains a significant determinant of the collective action" (Harding 2007, 82). (3) *Corporate Identity.* This takes for granted the corporate actor and their agency, over and against the agency of flesh and blood (i.e. tangible persons) and how, in terms of responsibility, this "… would vest in the collective or organisational agent, and not in any associated individuals" (Harding 2007, 82). Harding's typology is both clear and adheres to our practical reflections about how to approach crime. The key points we noted in relation to holding corporate actors criminally responsible were (1) establishing an underlying structure and (2) noting a capacity for internal decision making.

In the final section, we addressed two real-world examples of group criminality—war crimes, notably in relation to the SS-Einsatzgrupen Trial, and the matter of terrorism. We also addressed how to understand the phenomenon of the street gang criminologically. In dealing with Nazi war criminals we went through various arguments about responsibility, especially in relation to acting under military order in war time and in terms of the overall structure of a murderous organisation where no single person has complete control of the outcome. In looking at terrorism this was addressed in terms of exclusive and inclusive definitions of terrorism in the academic literature. We noted how the nature of the group may alter from place to place but that this is of less importance than the organising and structuring properties it has.

Finally, we looked at the phenomenon of the street gang by looking at the work of Becker and Cohan and more recent work by Hardie-Bick. Becker showed how the power of an externally applied label can affect the persons labelled, who then go on to live in terms of it. Becker's account is very much taken with the politics of the labelling process and how once applied it goes on to structure not just individuals but entire communities (Oddson and Bernburg 2017). The label is a sort of political category which is applied to *deviants* who are, in effect, simply recipients of dominant ideological determination. He understood how an individual person can be reduced to the level of a label recipient. What Becker understood is how the label operates below the level of the criminal law and how, cut off from statute, it has no obvious correlation with seriousness. In which case marijuana smoking, though objectively less serious than pension fund fraud, for example, receives far more public disapproval. He noted how, effectively, there would be no deviance without the application of a label in the first instance. He understood all too clearly how this labelling is characterised by issues of class, gender and race (Becker 1963, 18). Becker has a good understanding of how labels, characterised by issues of class, gender and race, are important in the development of alternative cultures. Stan Cohen was an intellectual colossus but his early work on moral panic and deviancy amplification is, arguably, his most well-read. His *Folk Devils and Moral Panics* (1973), along with the notion of the *moral panic* elucidated in it, are still central to any serious study of gangs. Cohen explained how comparatively small transgressions can be blown up in the media into moral panics, something Stuart Hall built on in *Policing the Crisis: Mugging, the State and Law and Order* (1978) which demonstrated how black youths were constructed as highly criminal by the popular media, in the face of statistical evidence to the contrary. Cohen termed this sort of distorting media portrayal *deviancy amplification* and how it was often undertaken for little more than popular entertainment (Cohen 1973, 16, 138). A much more profound point is that wherever there is deviancy amplification there is also, necessarily, a distancing between the reality of the world as it is and how it is relayed to other through the mass media: both in terms of perpetrating well-worn tales of urban youths and street gangs and in the systematic failure to address white collar criminality and the crimes of the powerful (Ruggiero 2015). Moreover, Cohen shows us how crime becomes an everyday fact of our daily lives (Cohen 1973, 53; Brotherton 2015, 34–35). In the work of Becker and Cohen we note how essentially external factors structure deviance, and crime more generally, and how this external pressure, and exposure, alters the way persons live their lives. Hardie-Bick, on the other hand, takes off from the existential, largely internal, worlds of people. He builds on the work of the Marxist social philosopher and psychoanalyst, Erich Fromm, and the more recent work of Michael Hogg. Hardie-Bick notes how the gang, and the violence often associated with it, is better explained in terms of it being an escape from the estrangement and existential insecurity of the modern world, and how this also usually entails giving up a part of their own individuality (Hardie-Bick 2016, 1035). The emphasis upon existential themes is itself part of a broader movement within contemporary criminology (Lippens and Crewe 2009). Hardie-Bick, following Hogg, argues how in late capitalist economies there is often a direct connection between "self-uncertainty" and group identification (Hogg 2007, 2014). The modern world undermines the formation of primary bonds leaving them isolated and in a precarious existential state (Amatrudo 2015a, b, 979). Hardie-Bick understands the gang as primarily an escape from existential indeterminacy and the anxiety that springs from it (Hardie-Bick 2016, 1037). The gang gives its members a sense of identity and purpose and is rooted in more than their anxiety-ridden lives. Of course, Hardie-Bick shows how the allure of gang membership is chimerical and that once they join the gang this also results in its own anxieties, not of solidarity, but of the illegal, dangerous and violent life of the gang life itself (Hardie-Bick 2016, 1039). The work of Hardie-Bick points to a truism: joining a gang is driven by existential and psychological factors and joining it may give rise to risk, risk to the members themselves.

Bibliography

Amatrudo, A. (2015a). Unheimlichkeit: Alienated and Integrated Identities and Criminal Existence(s). *Law, Jurisprudence, Governance and Existential Indeterminacy: Onati Socio-Legal Series, 5*(3), 969–981.

Amatrudo, A. (2015b). Individuals and Groups of Individuals Breaking Laws. In D. Crewe & R. Lippens (Eds.), *What is Criminology About?* (pp. 105–122). Abingdon: Routledge.

Becker, H. (1963). *Outsiders*. New York: Free Press.

Bratman, M. (1999). *Faces of Intention: Selected Essays on Intention and Agency*. Cambridge: Cambridge University Press.

Brotherton, D. (2015). *Youth Street Gangs: A Critical Appraisal*. London: Routledge.

Cohen, S. (1973). *Folk Devils and Moral Panics*. St Albans: Paladin Press.

Gilbert, M. (2000). *Sociality and Responsibility: New Essays in Plural Subject Theory*. Lanham: Rowman and Littlefield.

Hall, S., et al. (1978). *Policing the Crisis: Mugging, the State, and Law and Order*. London: Macmillan.

Hardie-Bick, J. (2016). Escaping the Self: Identity, Group Identification and Violence. *The Politics and Jurisprudence of Group Offending: Onati Socio-Legal Series, 6*(4), 1032–1052.

Harding, C. (2007). *Criminal Enterprise: Individuals, Organisations and Criminal Responsibility*. Cullompton: Willan Press.

Harding, S. (2014). *Street Casino: Survival in Violent Street Gangs*. Bristol: Policy Press.

Hogg, M. (2007). Uncertainty-Identity Theory. *Advances in Experimental Social Psychology, 39*(1), 69–126.

Hogg, M. (2014). From Uncertainty to Extremism: Social Categorization and Identity Processes. *Current Directions in Psychological Science, 23*(5), 338–342.

Lippens, R., & Crewe, D. (2009). *Existentialist Criminology*. London: Routledge.

List, C., & Petit, P. (2011). *Group Agency: The Possibility, Design and Status of Corporate Agents*. Oxford: OUP.

Oddson, G., & Bernburg, J. (2017). Opportunity Beliefs and Class Differences in Subjective Status Injustice During the Great Icelandic Recession. *Acta Sociologica*. Published Online First: July 2017.

Parfit, D. (1984). *Reasons and Persons*. Oxford: OUP.

Pyrooz, D., Turanovic, J., Decker, S., & Wu, J. (2016). Taking Stock of the Relationship Between Gang Membership and Offending: A Meta-Analysis. *Criminal Justice and Behaviour, 34*(3), 365–397.

Rude, G. (1964). *The Crowd in History*. New York: Wiley & Sons.

Ruggiero, V. (2015). *Power and Crime*. London: Routledge.

Smithson, H., Ralphs, R., & Williams, P. (2013). Used and Abused: The Problematic Usage of Gang Terminology in the United Kingdom and Its Implications for Ethnic Minority Youth. *British Journal of Criminology, 53*(1), 113–128.

Squires, P. (2016). *Voodoo Liability*: Joint Enterprise Prosecution as an Aspect of Intensified Criminalisation. *The Politics and Jurisprudence of Group Offending: Onati Socio-Legal Series, 6*(4), 937–956.

rua Wall, I. (2016). The Law of Crowds. *Legal Studies, 36*(3), 395–414.

Bibliography

Amatrudo, A. (2010). Being Lucky and Being Deserving and Distribution. *Heythrop Journal, 51*(1), 658–669.

Amatrudo, A. (2015a). Unheimlichkeit: Alienated and Integrated Identities and Criminal Existence(s). *Law, Jurisprudence, Governance and Existential Indeterminacy: Onati Socio-Legal Series, 5*(3), 969–981.

Amatrudo, A. (2015b). Individuals and Groups of Individuals Breaking Laws. In D. Crewe & R. Lippens (Eds.), *What is Criminology About?* (pp. 105–122). Abingdon: Routledge.

Amatrudo, A. (2016). Applying Analytical Reasoning to Clarify Intention and Responsibility in Joint Enterprise Cases. *The Politics and Jurisprudence of Group Offending: Onati Socio-Legal Series, 6*(4), 920–936.

Amatrudo, A. (2017). *Social Censure and Critical Criminology: After Sumner.* Basingstoke: Palgrave Macmillan.

Amatrudo, A., & Blake, L. (2015). *Human Rights and the Criminal Justice System.* London: Routledge.

Anderson, K. (1994). Nuremberg Sensibility. *Harvard Human Rights Journal, 7*(3), 281–295.

Andrew, E. (1983, September). Class in Itself and Class Against Capital: Karl Marx and His Classifers. *Canadian Journal of Political Science/Revue canadienne de science politique, 16*(3), 577–584.

© The Author(s) 2018
A. Amatrudo, *Criminal Actions and Social Situations,*
https://doi.org/10.1057/978-1-137-45731-8

Arnold, D. (2006). Corporate Moral Agency. *Midwest Studies in Philosophy, 30*(1), 279–291.

Arrigo, B., & Williams, C. (2009). Existentialism and the Criminology of the Shadow. In R. Lippens & D. Crewe (Eds.), *Existentialist Criminology* (pp. 222–245). London: Routledge.

Bauman, Z. (2000). *Liquid Modernity*. Cambridge: Polity Press.

Beck, U. (1998). *Risk Society: Towards a New Modernity*. London: Sage.

Becker, H. (1963). *Outsiders*. New York: Free Press.

Becker, H. (1974). Labelling Theory Reconsidered. In P. Rock & M. McIntosh (Eds.), *Deviance and Social Control*. London: Tavistock Press.

Bedau, H. A. (1978). Retribution and the Theory of Punishment. *Journal of Philosophy, 75*(2), 601–620.

Bentham. J. (1982). In J. H. Burns & H. L. A. Hart (Eds.), *An Introduction to the Principles of Morals and Legislation*. London: Methuen.

Blake, L. (2008). Hybrid Bills and Human Rights: The Parliament Square Litigation 2002–2007. *Kings Law Journal, 19*, 183–192.

Blickle, G., Schlegel, A., Fassbender, P., & Klein, U. (2006). Some Personality Correlates of Business White-Collar Crime. *Applied Psychology: An International Review, 55*(2), 220–223.

Bloxham, D. (2004). *Genocide on Trial*. Oxford: OUP.

Bosco, D. (2014). *Rough Justice; The International Criminal Court's Battle to Fix the World, One Prosecution at a Time*. Oxford: OUP.

Bowling, B., & Phillips, C. (2007). Disproportionate and Discriminatory: Reviewing the Evidence on Police Stop and Search. *Modern Law Review, 70*(6), 936–961.

Bratman, M. (1984). Two Faces of Intention. *The Philosophical Review, 93*(3), 375–405.

Bratman, M. (1987). *Intentions, Plans and Practical Reason*. Cambridge: Harvard University Press.

Bratman, M. (1992). Shared Cooperative Activity. *The Philosophical Review, 101*(2), 327–341.

Bratman, M. (1993). Shared Intention. *Ethics, 104*(1), 97–113.

Bratman, M. (1999). *Faces of Intention: Selected Essays on Intention and Agency*. Cambridge: Cambridge University Press.

Brocas, I., Camerer, C., Carrillo, J., & Wang, S. (2014). Imperfect Choice or Imperfect Attention: Understanding Strategic Thinking in Private Information Games. *Review of Economic Studies, 81*(3), 944–970.

Brotherton, D. (2007). Beyond Social Reproduction: Bringing Resistance Back Into the Theory of Gangs. *Theoretical Criminology, 12*(1), 55–77.

Brotherton, D. (2015). *Youth Street Gangs: A Critical Appraisal*. London: Routledge.

Brown, S. (2006). The Criminology of Hybrids: Rethinking Crime and Law in Techno-social Networks. *Theoretical Criminology, 10*(2), 223–244.

Brownlie, I. (2003). *Principles of Public International Law*. Oxford: OUP.

Buscher, F. (1989). *The United States War Crimes Trial Program in Germany, 1946–1955*. New York: Greenwood Press.

Bush, J. (2017). Nuremberg and Beyond. *Loyola LA International and Comparative Law Review, 259*(39), 259–286.

de la Calle, L., & Sanchez-Cuenca, I. (2011). What We Talk About When We Talk About Terrorism. *Politics and Society, 39*(3), 451–472.

Carter, D. (2012). A Blessing or a Curse? State Support for Terrorist Groups. *International Organization, 66*(1), 129–151.

Cassese, A. (2003). *International Criminal Law*. Oxford: OUP.

Cassese, A. (2005). *International Law*. Oxford: OUP.

Cesarani, D. (2005). *Eichmann: His Life and Crimes*. London: Vintage.

Cloward, R., & Ohlin, L. (1960). *Delinquency and Opportunity: A Theory of Delinquent Gangs*. New York: Free Press.

Cohen, S. (1971). *Images of Deviance*. Harmondsworth: Penguin Books.

Cohen, S. (1973). *Folk Devils and Moral Panics*. St Albans: Paladin Press.

Cohen, S. (1985). *Visons of Social Control: Crime, Punishment and Classification*. Cambridge: Polity Press.

Cohen, S., & Young, J. (1973). *The Manufacture of News: Deviance, Social Problems and the Mass Media*. London: Constable.

Coleman, J. (1982). *The Asymmetric Society: Organizational Actors, Corporate Power and the Irrelevance of Persons*. New York: Syracuse University Press.

Colman, A. (2003). Co-operation, Psychological Game Theory and Limitations of Rationality in Social Interation. *Behavioral and Brain Sciences, 26*(2), 139–153.

Coogan, T. P. (2000). *The I.R.A.* London: Harper Collins.

Cotte, S., & Hayward, K. (2011). The Terrorist (E)Motives: The Existential Attractions of Terrorism. *Studies in Conflict and Terrorism, 34*(12), 963–986.

Crenshaw, M. (1991). How Terror Declines. *Terrorism and Political Violence, 3*(1), 69–87.

Crewe, D. (2013). *Becoming Criminal: The Socio-Cultural Origins of Law, Transgression and Deviance*. Basingstoke: Palgrave Macmillan.

Crewe, D. (2016). Gang: Culture, Eidos and Process. *The Politics and Jurisprudence of Group Offending: Onati Socio-Legal Series, 6*(4), 999–1015.

Dan-Cohen, M. (1994). Between Selves and Collectivities: Towards a Jurisprudence of Identity. *University of Chicago Law Review, 61*(4), 1213–1243.

Davis, M. (1983). How to Make the Punishment Fit the Crime. *Ethics, 93*(2), 726–752.

Drury, J., & Reicher, S. (2000). Collective Action and Psychological Change: The Emergence of New Social Identities. *British Journal of Social Psychology, 39*(4), 579–604.

Duff, R. A. (1986). *Trials and Punishment.* Cambridge: Cambridge University Press.

Earl, H. (2009). *The Nuremberg SS-Einsatzgruppen Trial, 1945–1958: Atrocity Law and History.* New York: Cambridge University Press.

Earl, H. (2013a). Prosecuting Genocide Before the Genocide Convention: Raphael Lemkin and the Nuremberg Trials, 1945–1949. *Journal of Genocide Research, 15*(3), 317–338.

Earl, H. (2013b). Beweise, Zeugen, Narrative: Der Einsatzgruppen Prozess und seine Wirkung auf die historische Forschung zur Genese der Endlösung. In K. C. Priemel & A. Stiller (Eds.), *NMT. Nürnberger Militärtribunale zwischen Geschichte, Gerechigkeit und Rechtschöpfung* (pp. 127–157). Springer.

Erskine, T. (2003). *Can Institutions Have Responsibilities?* Basingstoke: Palgrave Macmillan.

Feinberg, J. (1970). *Doing and Deserving.* Princeton: Princeton University Press.

Ferran, E. (1999). *Company Law and Corporate Finance.* Oxford: OUP.

Finnis, F. (1980). *Natural Law and Natural Rights.* Oxford: Clarendon Press.

Fisse, B., & Braithwaite, J. (1993). *Corporations, Crime and Accountability.* Cambridge: Cambridge University Press.

Fleurbaev, M. (2015). Division of Labour in Policy Evaluation: Is There a Role for Normative Analysis. *The Good Society, 24*(1), 73–85.

French, P. (1979). The Corporation as a Moral Person. *American Philosophical Quarterly, 16*(3), 207–215.

French, P. (1984). *Collective and Corporate Personality.* New York: Columbia University Press.

French, P. (1992). *Responsibility Matters.* Lawrence: University Press of Kansas.

Fromm, E. (1941). *Escape From Freedom.* New York: Henry Holt & Company.

Gadirov, J. (2013). Casual Responsibility International Criminal Law. *International Criminal Law Review, 15*(5), 970–987.

Gearey, A., Morrison, W., & Jago, R. (2013). *The Politics of the Common Law: Perspectives, Rights, Processes, Institutions.* London: Routledge.

Geras, N. (2015). *Crimes Against Humanity: Birth of a Concept*. Manchester: Manchester University Press.

Gerwirth, A. (1978). *Reason and Morality*. Chicago: Chicago University Press.

Gilbert, M. (1992). *On Social Facts*. Princeton: Princeton University Press.

Gilbert, M. (1996). *Living Together: Rationality, Sociality and Obligation*. Lanham: Rowman and Littlefield.

Gilbert, M. (1999). Obligation and Joint Commitment. *Utilitas, 11*(2), 143–163.

Gilbert, M. (2000). *Sociality and Responsibility: New Essays in Plural Subject Theory*. Lanham: Rowman and Littlefield.

Gilbert, M. (2006). Rationality in Collective Action. *Philosophy of the Social Sciences, 36*(1), 3–17.

Goldhagen, D. (1996). *Hitler's Willing Executioners: Ordinary Germans and the Holocaust*. New York: Alfred Knopf.

Goldie, P. (2000). *The Emotions: A Philosophical Exploration*. Oxford: Clarendon Press.

Gordon, R. (2000). Criminal Business Organisations, Street Gangs and 'Wanna Be' Groups: A Vancouver Perspective. *Canadian Journal of Criminology and Criminal Justice, 42*(1), 39–60.

Gowa, J., & Mansfield, E. (2004). Alliances, Imperfect Markets and Major-Power Trade. *International Organisation, 58*(2), 775–805.

Grant, J. (2014). Riots in the UK: Morality, Social Imaginaries and Conditions of Possibility. *New Political Science, 36*(3), 311–329.

Green, A., & McGourlay, C. (2015). The Wolf Packs in Our Midst and Other Products of Joint Enterprise Prosecutions. *The Journal of Criminal Law, 79*(4), 280–297.

Guilfoos, T., & Duus Pape, A. (2016). Predicting Human Cooperation in the Prisoner's Dilemma Using a Case-Based Decision Theory. *Theory and Decision, 80*(1), 1–32.

Gupta, A., Briscoe, F., & Hambrick, D. (2017). Red, Blue, and Purple Firms: Organizational Political Ideology and Corporate Social Responsibility. *Strategic Management Journal, 38*(5), 1018–1040.

Hall, S., et al. (1978). *Policing the Crisis: Mugging, the State, and Law and Order*. London: Macmillan.

Hallsworth, S. (2013). *The Gang and Beyond: Interpreting Violent Street Worlds*. London: Palgrave Macmillan.

Hallsworth, S., & Young, T. (2008). Gang Talk and Gang Talkers. *Crime, Media and Culture, 4*(2), 175–195.

Hardie-Bick, J. (2016). Escaping the Self: Identity, Group Identification and Violence. *The Politics and Jurisprudence of Group Offending: Onati Socio-Legal Series, 6*(4), 1032–1052.

Harding, C. (2007). *Criminal Enterprise: Individuals, Organisations and Criminal Responsibility.* Cullompton: Willan Press.

Harding, S. (2014). *Street Casino: Survival in Violent Street Gangs.* Bristol: Policy Press.

Hart, H. L. A. (1968). *Punishment and Responsibility: Essays in the Philosophy of Law.* Oxford: OUP.

Hart, H. L. A., & Honore, A. (1968). *Causation in the Law.* Oxford: OUP.

Hayward, K., & Yar, M. (2006). The 'Chav' Phenomenon: Consumption, Media and the Construction of a New Underclass. *Crime, Media and Culture, 2*(1), 9–28.

Hinton, E. (2016). *From the War on Poverty to the War on Crime: The Making of Mass Incarceration in America.* Cambridge: Harvard University Press.

von Hirsch, A. (1978). Proportionality and Desert: A Reply to Bedau. *Journal of Philosophy, 75*(2), 622–624.

von Hirsch, A. (1985). *Past or Future Crimes?* Manchester: Manchester University Press.

von Hirsch, A. (1990). The Politics of Just Deserts. *Canadian Journal of Criminology, 397*(32), 407–409.

von Hirsch, A. (1996). *Censure and Sanctions.* Oxford: Clarendon Press.

HMIC. (2009). *Adapting to Protest: Nurturing a British Model of Policing.* London: HMIC.

Hmoud, M. (2013). Are New Principles Really Needed? The Potential of the Established Distinction Between Responsibility for Attacks by Nonstate Actors and the Law of Self-Defence. *American Journal of International Law, 107*(3), 576–579.

Hobsbawm, E. (1964). *Primitive Rebels.* Manchester: Manchester University Press.

Hodgson, S., & Tadros, V. (2013). The Impossibility of Defining Terrorism. *New Criminal Law Review, 16*(3), 494–526.

Hogg, M. (2007). Uncertainty-Identity Theory. *Advances in Experimental Social Psychology, 39*(1), 69–126.

Hogg, M. (2014). From Uncertainty to Extremism: Social Categorization and Identity Processes. *Current Directions in Psychological Science, 23*(5), 338–342.

Horgan, J., & Taylor, M. (1999). Playing the 'Green Card' – Financing the Provisional IRA. *Terrorism and Political Violence, 11*(2), 1–38.

Hurley, S. (1989). *Natural Reasons*. Oxford: OUP.

Ilan, J. (2015). *Understanding Street Culture: Poverty, Crime, Youth and Cool*. London: Palgrave Macmillan.

Jacques, S., & Wright, R. (2015). *Code of the Suburb: Inside the World of Young Middle-Class Drug Dealing*. Chicago: Chicago University Press.

Jayasingh, S., & Eze, U. (2015). An Empirical Analysis of Consumer Behavioral Intention Towards Mobile Coupons in Malaysia. *International Journal of Business and Information, 4*(2), 221–242.

Jeßberger, F. (2016). Corporate Involvement in Slavery and Criminal Responsibility Under International Law. *Journal of International Criminal Justice, 14*(2), 327–341.

Katz, J., & Jackson-Jacobs, C. (2004). The Criminologist's Gang. In C. Sumner (Ed.), *Blackwell Companion to Criminology* (pp. 91–124). Oxford: Blackwell.

Kelsen, H. (1999). *General Theory of Law and State*. Cambridge: Harvard University Press.

Kershaw, I. (2008). *Hitler, The Germans and the Final Solution*. New Haven: Yale University Press.

Kershaw, I. (2015). *To Hell and Back: Europe 1914– 1949*. London: Allen Lane.

Kistner, U. (2015). Common Purpose: The Crowd and the Public. *Law Critique, 26*, 27–43.

Klein, M., & Maxon, C. (2006). *Street Gang Patterns and Policies*. Oxford: OUP.

Knight, S., Goold, M., & Elliott, E. (2013). New Threat to the Right to Protest: Stephen Knight on the New Arrest Tactic to Include Legal Observers and Michael Goold and Emily Elliott on an Important Victory in the High Court Against the Met Police and Its Kettling Actions. *Socialist Lawyer, 65*(October), 14–17.

Krebs, B. (2015). Mens Rea in Joint Enterprise; A Role for Endorsement? *Cambridge Law Journal, 74*(30), 480–504.

Kutz, C. (2000). *Complicity: Ethics and Law for a Collective Age*. Cambridge: Cambridge University Press.

Landsman, S. (2005). *Crimes of the Holocaust: The Law Confronts Hard Cases*. Philadelphia: University of Pennsylvania Press.

Langerbein, H. (2004). *Hitler's Death Squads: The Logic of Mass Murder*. College Station: Texas A&M University Press.

Lederman, E. (2000). Models for Imposing Corporate Criminal Liability: From Adoption and Imitation Towards Aggregation and the Search for Self-Identity. *Buffalo Criminal Law Review, 4*(1), 641–708.

Lemert, E. (1951). *Social Pathology*. New York: McGraw-Hill.

Lemkin, R. (1946). Genocide. *American Scholar, 2*(15), 227–270.

Levi, M. (2002). The Organization of Serious Crime. In M. Maguire, R. Morgan, & R. Reiner (Eds.), *The Oxford Handbook of Criminology* (3rd ed., pp. 878–913). Oxford: OUP.

Lippens, R., & Crewe, D. (2009). *Existentialist Criminology*. London: Routledge.

List, C., & Petit, P. (2011). *Group Agency: The Possibility, Design and Status of Corporate Agents*. Oxford: OUP.

Lobban, M. (1990). From Seditious Libel to Unlawful Assembly; Peterloo and the Changing Face of Political Crime c.1770–1820. *Oxford Journal of Legal Studies, 10*(3), 307–352.

Locke, J. (1975). *An Essay Concerning Human Understanding*. Oxford: OUP.

Longerich, P. (2012). *Heinrich Himmler*. Oxford: OUP.

Longmire, S., & Longmire, J. (2008). Redefining Terrorism: Why Mexican Drug Trafficking Is More Than Just Organized Crime. *Journal of Strategic Security, 1*(1), 35–51.

Luhmann, N. (1984). *Soziale Systeme: Grundriß einer allgemeinen Theorie*. Frankfurt: Suhrkamp.

Mackay, W. (2004). *Erskine May's Treatise on the Law, Privileges and Usage of Parliament* (23rd ed.). London: Butterworths.

Mackie, J. L. (1985). *Persons and Values*. Oxford: Clarendon Press.

Marrus, M. (2000). *The Holocaust in History*. Toronto: Key Porter Press.

Mayeda, D., Chesney-Lind, M., & Koo, J. (2001). Talking Story with Hawaii's Youth: Confronting Violent and Sexualized Perceptions of Ethnicity and Gender. *Youth and Society, 33*(1), 99–128.

McDonald, M. (1987). The Personless Paradigm. *University of Toronto Law Journal, 37*(212), 219–220.

Morgan, P. (2017). Certainty in Vicarious Liability: A Quest for a Chimera? *Cambridge Law Journal, 75*(2), 202–205.

Morris, H. (1968). Persons and Punishment. *The Monist, 52*(4), 475–501.

Morrison, S. (2015). Membership Crime v. The Right to Assemble. *John Marshall Law Review, 48*(3), 729–755.

Murphy, J. (1987). Does Kant Have a Theory of Punishment? *Columbia Law Review, 87*(3), 509–542.

Norrie, A. (1991). A Critique of Criminal Causation. *Modern Law Review, 54*(5), 685–701.

Oddson, G., & Bernburg, J. (2017). Opportunity Beliefs and Class Differences in Subjective Status Injustice During the Great Icelandic Recession. *Acta Sociologica*. Published Online First: July 2017.

Panfil, V. (2014). Better Left Unsaid? The Role of Agency in Queer Criminological Research. *Critical Criminology, 22*(1), 99–111.

Parfit, D. (1984). *Reasons and Persons.* Oxford: OUP.

Persico, J. (2000). *Nuremberg: Infamy on Trial.* London: Penguin Books.

Pitts, J. (2014). Who Dunnit? Gangs, Joint Enterprise, Bad Character and Duress. *Youth and Policy, 113*(1), 48–59.

Pogany, I. (1997). *Righting Wrongs in Eastern Europe.* Manchester: Manchester University Press.

Pontell, H., Black, N., William, K., & Geis, G. (2014). Too Big to Fail, Too Powerful to Jail? On the Absence of Criminal Prosecutions after the 2008 Financial Meltdown. *Crime, Law and Social Change, 61*(1), 1–13.

Price, B. (2012). Targeting Top Terrorists: How Leadership Decapitation Contributes to Counterterrorism. *International Security, 36*(4), 9–46.

Pyrooz, D., Turanovic, J., Decker, S., & Wu, J. (2016). Taking Stock of the Relationship Between Gang Membership and Offending: A Meta-Analysis. *Criminal Justice and Behaviour, 34*(3), 365–397.

Ratner, S. (2001). Corporations and Human Rights; A Theory of Legal Responsibility. *Yale Law Journal, 111*(93), 443–545.

Reiner, R. (2016). *Crime.* Cambridge: Polity Press.

Rossino, A. (2003). *Hitler Strikes Poland: Blitzkrieg, Ideology and Atrocity.* Lawrence: University of Kansas Press.

Roth, A. (2003). Practical Inter-Subjectivity. In F. Schmitt (Ed.), *Socializing Metaphysics; The Nature of Social Reality* (pp. 65–69). New York: Rowman & Littlefield.

Roth, A. (2004). Shared Agency and Contralateral Commitments. *The Philosophical Review, 113*(3), 359–410.

Rude, G. (1964). *The Crowd in History.* New York: Wiley & Sons.

Ruggiero, V. (2015). *Power and Crime.* London: Routledge.

Rutherford, J. (2014). *Combat and Genocide on the Eastern Front.* Cambridge: Cambridge University Press.

Sadurski, W. (1985). *Giving Desert Its Due.* Lancaster/Dordrecht: Springer.

Salsa, S. (2016). *Partial Differential Equations: From Modelling to Theory.* London: Springer.

Sanchez-Brigado, R. E. (2010). *Groups, Rules and Legal Practice.* London: Springer.

Schabas, W. (2004). *An Introduction to the International Criminal Court.* Cambridge: Cambridge University Press.

Schmid, A., & Jongman, A. (1988). *Political Terrorism: A Guide to Actors, Authors, Concepts, Databases, Theories and Literature.* New Brunswick: Transaction Press.

Searle, J. (1980). The Intentionality of Intention and Action. *Cognitive Science, 4*(1), 47–70.

Searle, J. (1997). Responses to the Critics of the Construction of Social Reality. *Philosophy and Phenomenological Research, 57*(2), 449–458.

Sen, A. (2006). *Identity and Violence: The Illusion of Destiny.* New York: Norton.

Sergi, A. (2014). Organised Crime in Criminal Law: Conspiracy and Membership Offences in Italian, English and International Frameworks. *Kings Law Journal, 25*(2), 185–200.

Sheehy, P. (2006). *The Reality of Social Groups.* Chippenham: Ashgate.

Simester, A., & Sullivan, G. (2003). *Criminal Law: Theory and Doctrine.* Oxford: Hart.

Slapper, G., & Tombs, S. (1999). *Corporate Crime.* London: Longman.

Smithson, H., Ralphs, R., & Williams, P. (2013). Used and Abused: The Problematic Usage of Gang Terminology in the United Kingdom and Its Implications for Ethnic Minority Youth. *British Journal of Criminology, 53*(1), 113–128.

Squires, P. (2016). *Voodoo Liability*: Joint Enterprise Prosecution as an Aspect of Intensified Criminalisation. *The Politics and Jurisprudence of Group Offending: Onati Socio-Legal Series, 6*(4), 937–956.

Stott, C., & Drury, J. (2000). Crowds, Context and Identity: Dynamic Categorization Processes in the Poll Tax Riot. *Human Relations, 53*(2), 247–273.

Sugden, R. (2000). Team Preferences. *Economics and Philosophy, 16*(2), 175–204.

Sumner, C. (1994). *The Sociology of Deviance: An Obituary.* Buckingham: Open University Press.

Surowiecki, J. (2004). *The Wisdom of Crowds.* London: Abacus Books.

Taylor, M. (1987). *The Possibility of Cooperation.* Cambridge: Cambridge University Press.

Taylor, T. (1992). *The Anatomy of the Nuremberg Trials: A Personal Memoir.* Toronto: Little, Brown & Co.

Tenenbaum, J. (1955). The Einsatzgruppen. *Jewish Social Studies, 17*(1), 43–64.

Tombs, S., & Whyte, D. (2015). Counterblast: Crime, Harm and the State-Corporate Nexus. *Howard Journal of Criminal Justice, 54*(1), 91–95.

Tosun, J., Koos, S., & Shore, J. (2016). Co-governing Common Goods: Interaction Patterns of Private and Public Actors. *Policy and Society, 35*(1), 1–12.

Tuomela, R. (2005). We-intentions Revisited. *Philosophical Studies, 125*(3), 327–369.

Tuomela, R. (2007). *The Philosophy of Sociality: The Shared Point of View*. Oxford: OUP.

Varian, H. (1987). *Intermediate Microeconomics*. London: W.W. Norton Publishers.

Wahl, J. (2016). The Problem of Choice. *Journal of French and Francophone Philosophy, 24*(1), 224–258.

rua Wall, I. (2016). The Law of Crowds. *Legal Studies, 36*(3), 395–414.

Warren, M. (1997). *Moral Status*. Oxford: Clarendon Press.

Weinberg, L. (1991). Turning to Terror: The Conditions Under Which Political Parties Turn to Terrorist Activities. *Comparative Politics, 23*(4), 423–438.

Wells, C. (2001). *Corporations and Criminal Responsibility*. Oxford: OUP.

Williams, P., & Clarke, B. (2016). *Dangerous Associations: Joint Enterprise, Gangs and Racism*. London: Centre for Crime and Justice Studies.

Wilson, J. Q. (1973). *Political Organizations*. New York: Basic Books.

Xiao, E., & Kunreuther, H. (2012). *Punishment and Cooperation in Stochastic Social Dilemmas* (Wharton NBER Working Papers, Number 18458, pp. 1–38).

Young, J. (2007). *The Vertigo of Late Modernity*. London: Sage.

Young, L. (2014). *The Young Review: Improving Outcomes for Young Black And/Or Muslim Men in the Criminal Justice System*. London: Ministry of Justice.

Index[1]

---

[1]Note: Page numbers followed by 'n' refer to notes.

© The Author(s) 2018
A. Amatrudo, *Criminal Actions and Social Situations*,
https://doi.org/10.1057/978-1-137-45731-8

Printed in the United States
By Bookmasters